TERTULLIAN · CYPRIAN · ORIGEN

On the Lord's Prayer

T0338988

ST VLADIMIR'S SEMINARY PRESS
Popular Patristics Series
Number 29

The Popular Patristics Series published by St Vladimir's Seminary Press provides readable and accurate translations of a broad range of early Christian literature to a wide audience—from students of Christian history to lay Christians reading for spiritual benefit. Recognized scholars in their fields provide short but comprehensive and clear introductions to the material. The texts include classics of Christian literature, thematic volumes, collections of homilies, letters on spiritual counsel, and poetical works from a variety of geographical contexts and historical backgrounds. The mission of the series is to mine the riches of the early Church and to make these treasures available to all.

Series Editor
BOGDAN BUCUR

Associate Editor
IGNATIUS GREEN

* * *

Series Editor
1999–2020
JOHN BEHR

TERTULLIAN

CYPRIAN

ORIGEN

On the Lord's Prayer

Translated and introduced,
With brief annotations by

ALISTAIR STEWART-SYKES

ST VLADIMIR'S SEMINARY PRESS
CRESTWOOD, NEW YORK

Library of Congress Cataloging-in-Publication Data

On the Lord's prayer / Tertullian, Cyprian, Origen ; translated and
introduced, with brief annotations, by Alistair Stewart-Sykes.

      p.   cm.— (St. Vladimir's Seminary Press popular patristics series)
      ISBN 0-88141-261-9

      1. Lord's prayer. I. Stewart-Sykes, Alistair. II. Tertullian, ca. 160–CA. 230.
De oratione. English.   III. Cyprian, Saint, Bishop of Carthage. De domenica
oratione. English.   IV. Origen. De oratione. English.   V. Series

   BV 230.O5 2004
   226.9'606—dc22

                                     2004006780

ISBN-13: 978-0-88141-261-1
ISBN-10: 0-88141-261-9

COPYRIGHT © 2004

ST VLADIMIR'S SEMINARY PRESS

575 Scarsdale Rd., Crestwood, NY 10707
1-800-204-2665
www.svspress.com

ISBN 978-0-88141-261-1

PRINTED IN THE UNITED STATES OF AMERICA

For Peter
with love

Table of Contents

Preface

The works presented here are the three ante-Nicene treatises on prayer that have been bequeathed to us. There is a certain diversity in the works. For whereas Tertullian and Cyprian not only have an obvious relationship, their works are likewise similar, and derive from the same liturgical context, for all of which reasons they share an introduction. Origen's work is very different in character, and comes from a different part of the Empire, and therefore is introduced separately. Yet given the diversity of early Christianity and the divergent purpose of these works, as Richard Stuckwisch, in his summary and descriptive article on these treatises ("Principles of Christian Prayer from the Third Century," *Worship* 71 [1997]: 2–19) points out, the extent of the material which they hold in common is quite remarkable. In particular, each sees the Lord's Prayer as the model and summit of all Christian prayer. And each has much to teach us.

For this reason, like my earlier translation of *On Pascha* in this series, the following translations are intended for a general, rather than a specialist, audience. With the needs of this audience in mind I have sought clarity above all else, and this is the standard on which I would that they be judged; I understand my task as that of producing prose which might have been written in English, and for this reason I have rearranged periods, transposed passives to actives (and vice versa), and sat lightly on the sequence of tenses. I have attempted to use inclusive language, though have occasionally been defeated. If an audience of undergraduates, general readers, and parochial clergy profit from the reading of these fathers through this medium, then their interpreter will have succeeded.

In translating Tertullian I have employed the text presented by Evans in *Tertullian's Tract on the Prayer*. In translating Cyprian I have employed that of Réveillaud, though this text has several typographical errors (including, at one point, the omission of an entire line), which has meant recourse to Hartel. The translation of Origen is based on the text provided by Koetschau among the Griechische Christliche Schriftsteller. However, I have departed from Koetschau's readings occasionally. When I have done this it is indicated in a footnote. The work is extant in its entirety in a single manuscript, codex Holmiensis in Cambridge, and because of the poor state of the text, editorial suggestions are widespread and inevitable. Among those to which allusion is made in the notes are those of Delarue, who published an edition in France in 1733 (which was subsequently reproduced by Migne), Bentley, whose work on the text in the seventeenth century was largely adopted by Delarue, and Anglus. Anglus is the pseudonym for an anonymous Englishman of the seventeenth century, who made numerous suggestions for emendation of the text, as well as suggestions concerning its interpretation which were first published in an edition of 1728, and were subsequently included in an appendix to the edition of Delarue. I will confess to a certain affection toward this anonymous divine, and attraction to the idea that he might have been Herbert Thorndike. I will also confess having learnt much, and having often borrowed terms and phrases, from those Anglicans who have published translations of these works before me: Evans of Tertullian, Jay of Origen, and Bindley of Cyprian, each published by SPCK in 1953, 1954, and 1914 respectively. It is gratifying indeed to be treading in the way marked by a former archdeacon of Barbados and Principal of Codrington College, and Origen would reproach me did I not make it clear that I have been assisted throughout by the prayers of the saints (among whom Bindley and Thorndike are surely numbered) and the ministrations of the angels.

Inevitably I have accrued debts along the way to those living still on this earth, as well as those who await the resurrection, for which this publication can provide only partial discharge. Once again I pay tribute to the editor of this series, Fr John Behr, for his continued patience. Though I had planned the work for some time, I was encouraged to begin it by speaking to a group of parishioners on the Lord's Prayer, and once embarked found numerous occasions to apply the insights gained in translating these texts in my parochial work, both pastoral and catechetical, and so I extend my thanks to all the people of my parishes. As I labored at this task Judy Newman was, once again, a veritable Epaphroditus, whilst Fr Barrie Bates has proved an Onesimus.

Finally, Peter has been very patient in waiting for *his* book. I hope he considers the wait worthwhile, even though it is a grown-up book without any pictures.

Sturminster Marshall Vicarage
On the Feast of St Antony of Egypt
2003

Note: Although Tertullian and Cyprian did not use the LXX, as did Origen, they did not use the Vulgate either, and so, for consistency, scriptural references have been given according to the LXX throughout.

Introduction to
Tertullian and Cyprian

Tertullian

For the life of Tertullian we are dependent upon one short account, which is of sufficient brevity that it may be quoted in full.[1]

> Tertullian the presbyter, now considered the chief of the Latin writers after Victor and Apollonius, was of the province of Africa and city of Carthage, his father being a proconsular centurion. This man of vigorous character flourished chiefly under Severus and Antoninus Caracalla, and wrote many volumes, which we shall not name since they are familiar to most people. I have seen at Concordia, which is a town in Italy, a certain Paul, an old man who claimed, when he was a young man, to have seen at Rome a secretary of the blessed Cyprian, by then of advanced age, who said that Cyprian would never let a day go by without reading Tertullian, and would often say: "Give me the master," by which he meant Tertullian. He was, until his middle years, a presbyter of the church, but afterwards, driven by the envy and abuse of the clergy of the Roman church, fell into the opinion of Montanus, to which, in many books, he referred as the "new prophecy." In particular he composed volumes against the church, *On Modesty*, *On*

[1]There is an earlier witness to Tertullian, namely Eusebius, *Ecclesiastical History* 2.2, but Eusebius is under the impression that he is a Roman and has nothing to say about him beyond quoting a short extract from his *Apology*.

Persecution, On Fasting, On Monogamy, six books *On
Ecstasy* and a seventh which he composed *Against Apollo-
nius.* He is said to have lived to feeble old age and to have
published many short works, which are not extant.
(Jerome *On Illustrious Men* 53)

Some of the points made here are borne out by Tertullian's own
works. That Tertullian was of a wealthy and influential background
is shown by his apparent education and rhetorical ability. There
are, however, two assertions that must be questioned in Jerome's
account.

The first point is the allegation that Tertullian left the catholic
church and joined a Montanist cult. Rankin marshalls impressive
reasons for reading the evidence in another way:[2] Tertullian never
encourages anybody to leave the catholic church, but rather
remained within the church and sought a more rigorous form of
Christianity within it. He is considered a teacher and master by
Cyprian, to whom schism was a fatal error—a status he would
hardly have received had he been himself a schismatic. Tertullian's
high view of Christian hierarchy, and his failure to recognize any
hierarchy apart from that of the catholic church, is entirely consonant with Cyprian's views, and Cyprian's own discourse on the
Lord's Prayer is frequently close to Tertullian's, which is an illustration of the extent to which he was indebted to the earlier figure, as
Jerome reports.

It would seem that Jerome has been led astray by his failure to
understand the nature of Christianity in North Africa in the third
century. As Tabbernee points out, the martyrdom of Perpetua and
Felicity indicates some "factional tension" in the Carthaginian
church,[3] but these martyrs nonetheless remain firmly loyal to the

---

[2]David Rankin, *Tertullian and the Church* (Cambridge: CUP, 1995), 27–51.

[3]W. Tabbernee, "Remnants of the New Prophecy: Literary and Epigraphical
Sources of the Montanist Movement," in E. A. Livingstone, ed., *Studia Patristica,* 21
(Leuven: Peeters, 1989), 193–201 at 196.

bishop Optatus. There is no question that Tertullian was favorably inclined in his later years toward the New Prophecy, but at this time there was no formal schism between Carthaginian followers of the New Prophecy and the catholic church, as the disagreement was contained within the church. At the time of Jerome it was no longer possible to be sympathetic to Montanism (as the New Prophecy came to be called) and yet faithful to the catholic church, and therefore Jerome has assumed that Tertullian left the catholic church in this period.

The reason for laboring this point is to enter a caveat against Evans' assertion that the work *On Prayer* must be an early work because it shows no trace of Montanism, and is loyally ecclesial.[4] We shall return to the literary history of the work below, but for the moment may observe that its attitudes are fundamentally conservative, as Tertullian pours scorn on various liturgical innovations entering the Carthaginian church at his time. It is the same conservative attitude which, we may suggest, led to his support of the New Prophecy which, both in its ethical rigorism and in its dependence on prophetic revelation, might be perceived as a neo-conservative movement within the African church of the early third century.

The second point made by Jerome which we must question is the statement that Tertullian was a presbyter; Tertullian's own statement in *Exhortation to Chastity* 7.3 stands in express denial of this: "Are we laypersons not also priests?"[5] Although Tertullian is, on the basis of this evidence, clearly not a presbyter, it may be possible to explain the manner in which the confusion arose by suggesting that Tertullian was a *senior*. The institution of *seniores* is unique to the African church; they are a group of lay elders who have responsibility for the management of the business of the church. The *seniores*

---

[4]E. Evans, *Tertullian's Tract on the Prayer* (London: SPCK, 1953), xi.

[5]As Rankin, *Tertullian*, 39, points out, there have been attempts to read this statement in such a way as it states the opposite, namely that Tertullian was a presbyter; however, not only is this a forced and impossible reading of the Latin, but the word *sacerdos*, which here is translated "priest," more normally applies to the bishop. Nobody has ever suggested that Tertullian was a bishop.

were not, however, presbyters, in that they were not ordained. The title, however, may lead to misunderstanding among those unfamiliar with African Christianity since this Latin title might easily be understood as a Latin word for presbyter. This is probably the source of Jerome's misunderstanding.

I have argued for the existence of this group elsewhere,[6] and may sum up the arguments presented there as follows:

1) The professionalization of presbyters, which occurs in the third century, is odd, were the presbyteral class a growth from the patron-elders known elsewhere. If, however, the patron-elders continue as *seniores*, and the *presbyteri* are a distinct institution from a distinct group, the problem disappears.

2) This is possible, given that there are references to the *seniores* in Tertullian and in the *Passion of Perpetua*, as well as a reference to "men of high standing" (*Graves viri*) who collaborate with the bishop in Cyprian's *Letter* 38.2.

3) *Seniores laici* emerge clearly in the fourth century. It is odd that a powerful lay class should emerge as the church becomes more clericalized, unless this lay class is an ancient institution.

4) *Seniores* is a Latin term, which has an equivalent in the term *antistes*, used of a bishop. *Presbyteri*, as a Greek term, may therefore be an importation.

The origin of these *seniores* is not known. It is possible that they derive from the elders of the synagogue,[7] or that they are a continuation of the practice of elders common in the pagan villages of the Maghreb.[8] Of the two possibilities it is more probable that the elders

[6]"Ordination Rites and Patronage Systems in Third-Century Africa," *Vigiliae Christianae*, 56 (2002): 115–130.

[7]So W.H.C. Frend, "The *seniores laici* and the Origins of the Church in North Africa," *JTS* n.s. 12 (1961): 280–284; G. Quispel, "African Christianity before Minucius Felix and Tertullian," in J. den Boeft and A.H.M. Kessels, eds., *Actus: studies in honour of H. L. W. Nelson* (Utrecht: Instituut voor klassieke Talen, 1982), 257–335 at 275–277.

[8]So Brent D. Shaw, "The Elders of Christian Africa," in *Mélanges offerts en hommage au Révérend Père Étienne Gareau* (Quebec: Éditions de l'Université d'Ottawa, 1982), 207–226 at 221–226.

of Maghrebi villages are the origin of this institution, as this is an indication of the manner in which the African church constructed itself as a contra-cultural institution through the adoption of patterns of leadership known from the pagan world, a phenomenon which I have also explored elsewhere.[9] It is only natural that Tertullian, as a person of wealth and education within the church, would find himself in this position, as, whatever the origin of the institution, this class would continue to represent the original patron-elders.

There are two points at which we may see the *seniores* in a liturgical context. First there is the picture of *seniores* in worship provided by the vision of Saturus in *The Passion of Perpetua*, in which the Lord is flanked by *seniores* and see this as representing the manner in which the bishop was seated in the assembly.[10] Secondly we may suggest that the gatherings after worship for the testing of prophecy[11] were undertaken by *seniores*.

Thus it is as *senior* that we should see Tertullian functioning within the church of Carthage, and as *senior* that we should understand him giving the address translated here which, we shall see, is an address to catechumens on the prayer which they are to make on coming out of the water. For since Tertullian is not ordained, it is hard to see on what basis, apart from being a *senior*, any layman might be selected to perform the task of instructing catechumens, both in this address and in that which he delivered on baptism to the same audience, those who are undergoing intense preparation.[12]

---

[9]"Catechumenate and Contra-Culture: The Social Process of Catechumenate in Third-Century Africa and its Development," *SVTQ* 47.3–4 (2003), 289–306.

[10]So Shaw, "Christian Elders," 209–210. Cf. Quispel, "African Christianity," 306, who imagines (*a priori*) a clash between the structures represented by the episcopate and the *seniores*.

[11]As described by W. Tabbernee, "To Pardon or Not to Pardon: North African Montanism and the Forgiveness of Sins" at http://divinity.library.vanderbilt.edu/burns/chroma/penance/pentabb.html.

[12]"Qui maxime formantur" (*On Baptism* 1).

Cyprian

We are well informed about Cyprian's life, at least after he became a Christian, not only as a result of his biography written by the deacon Pontius and the acts of his martyrdom but also as a result of his own writings, and in particular his extensive correspondence, which touches on many of the issues with which he dealt as bishop. Because of the historic importance of the events of his episcopate and the theological significance of the ecclesiology that was forged as a result of these events, much has been written on this subject.[13] Therefore only the briefest account of his life need be given here.

Pontius says little about Cyprian's life before he became a Christian, as the rebirth of baptism marked his true beginning. Cyprian himself reveals little about his previous existence, except to say that it was purposeless, but we may deduce both from the hints that are left and from Cyprian's subsequent conduct that he was wealthy, educated, and highborn. We also know that he was a convert, his conversion brought about through his friendship with Caecilius, an aged presbyter. Pontius reports that his catechumenate was brief as a result of the rapid progress that he made.[14] It is certainly true that a moral conversion to the contra-culture of Christianity took place, as Pontius reports that Cyprian, in his catechumenate, divested himself of whole estates for the benefit of the poor. Not only was his catechumenate brief, his time as a layman was likewise brief, as rapidly he was ordained presbyter and then elected and ordained bishop, apparently within two years of his conversion.[15] As a member of the patronal class who had renounced the way of life engendered by patronage, he was rapidly elected to a position in which he would exercise patronage within a contra-culture.

His episcopate was marked, however, by the outbreak of persecution under the Emperor Decius in 249. All persons in the empire

---

[13]The most thorough and readable discussion is that of J. Patout Burns, *Cyprian the Bishop* (New York: Routledge, 2002).

[14]Pontius *Life* 2.

[15]Pontius *Life* 3.

were obliged to offer sacrifice. At the beginning of 250 Cyprian went into hiding, believing that as a prominent Christian he might provide a focus for pagan hostility, and in order the better to run the affairs of his diocese. Even in this period, as the persecution quickly ran its course, a schism threatened on the basis of differing attitudes to those who had offered sacrifice. There were those who refused, known as confessors; those who had sacrificed; and a middle group, those who had obtained certificates stating that they had sacrificed when they had not actually done so. Cyprian was unwilling to determine a position on those who had thus lapsed until a council had considered such a matter, but his position was made difficult in that some of those who had sacrificed obtained letters from confessors on the basis of which they might be readmitted to the communion of the Church. This was possible because martyrs were believed to have a special access to God, and could promise that the effect of their prayers would be so efficacious in heaven that the earthly church would be obliged to follow suit. Clearly this would lead to conflict between the claims of the martyrs and the control of the bishop. The lapsed were clearly a powerful group within Carthage, and probably represented those of high economic status within the Christian community. At the end of the persecution, Cyprian describes those lapsed who ought to be doing penance as those overeating and dressing in fine clothes,[16] which, even allowing for rhetorical exaggeration, implies that this group was relatively wealthy. There is an inherent probability here, in that those with wealth would be more affected by the imperial demand for sacrifice, as they would more readily come to the attention of Roman authorities, whereas those of low economic status would not generally be troubled because they were less noticeable.

A council was finally able to meet in 251, and agreed to the principle that those who had lapsed should be readmitted only in danger of death, whereas those who had obtained certificates without sacrificing should be readmitted on the basis of penance already

[16]*On the Lapsed* 30.

undertaken. Inevitably this position did not satisfy either the rigorists
or the laxists, and by 252 there were two rival bishops in Carthage.
Although the rigorists made little headway in Carthage, the laxists
had support of leading presbyters, many of whom had opposed the
election of Cyprian (though the voice of the laity held sway in this
election). In the event, however, all the lapsed were readmitted in a
short period, as a further persecution was threatened, and as plague
raged in the city in that year. Readmission to communion on the basis
of evidence of penitence would not mean automatic salvation, but
would make it possible for those re-admitted to have a hearing at the
heavenly tribunal. Cyprian thus strengthened the cohesion of the
church, enabling it to face the renewed persecution.

Further controversy followed, as a dispute with the Roman
church then developed concerning the validity of baptisms admin-
istered outside the catholic church, an issue which arose as a result
of schisms in Rome resulting from the differing attitudes to those
who had lapsed in persecution. Rome recognized such baptisms,
requiring that those baptized outside the catholic church receive a
laying on of hands only, presumably in reconciliation,[17] whereas
Cyprian extended no recognition to these baptisms. In this he followed the decision reached by an earlier African council[18] and
exhibited his understanding that baptism, namely the forgiveness of
sins through the Holy Spirit, could only be conveyed through the
church that was the sole possessor of that Spirit.[19] The dispute was
unresolved when persecution broke out again in 257, in which he
was first exiled and then returned to Carthage where he was mar-
tyred in 258.

[17]A rite described by Cyprian at *Letter* 71.2.2. At 72.1.1, however, he seems to suggest that the hand-laying is the post-baptismal hand-laying given to confer the Holy
Spirit on the newly baptized. G. Clarke, *The Letters of Saint Cyprian* IV (New York:
Newman, 1989), 216, suggests that this is a muddying of the waters. On the ambigu-
ity of this action see especially M. Bévenot "Cyprian's Platform in the Rebaptism Controversy," *Heythrop Journal*, 19 (1978): 123–142 at 125–127.

[18]Reported by Cyprian at *Letter* 71.4.1.

[19]See a full explanation of this theory in *Letter* 69.1.11.

Deriving from Cyprian's struggles both with the Roman church and within Carthage is his thought concerning the role of the bishop in the church. Rather Cyprian does not define a role for the bishop, because the bishop himself personifies the church in each diocese. The episcopate is one, the local exercise of which is held by single bishops, each with the authority of the whole.[20] The aspect of each individual bishop's authority as part of a common episcopate is thought through against the background of the dispute with the Roman bishop, whereas the juridical function of the bishop within his diocese derives, as Evans points out, from the necessity of determining who of those who had lapsed might be readmitted to the church.[21] Most significant, however, is the manner in which Cyprian views the bishop as absolute governor within his diocese.[22] The significance of this point for the discourse translated here will be explored below. We may likewise observe, even from this treatise, how Cyprian considered unity to be an essential mark of the church, as even catechumens are warned of the danger of schism, with statements such as:

The one who is disruptive and disagreeable and is not at peace with the brothers, even though he be put to death for the name, shall not be able to escape the charge of hostility toward the brothers. (24)

and:

. . . thus it may also be understood how great a sin it is to tear apart unity and peace, because the Lord prayed for this very thing, desiring that his people should have life, knowing that discord does not enter the Kingdom of God. (30)

[20] *On Unity* 5.

[21] R. F. Evans, *One and Holy: The Church in Latin Patristic Thought* (London: SPCK, 1972), 48–49.

[22] Thus note his statements in *Letter* 59, that the bishop governs the church (59.2.2) and that all should obey the bishop in keeping with the teaching of Scripture (59.5.2).

This is sufficient to introduce the authors of these treatises. We may now turn to the treatises themselves.

The genesis of the African treatises on the Lord's prayer

At the time of Augustine the Lord's Prayer was taught to the cate-chumens at the conclusion of the catechumenate, in a ceremony that took place one week before the Easter vigil.[23] Grossi points out that this is an appropriate concluding point to the catechumenate, since at this point the catechumens have learnt of the unfolding of the his-tory of salvation and have been formed in the faith, and so are now taught how to pray, and given a summary in prayer of the Gospel.[24]

Since this is the time at which the final rite of exorcism and renunciation was given in the third century, and indeed continued to be given in the fifth century, it is possible that the delivery of the Lord's Prayer followed on from that rite of renunciation and exor-cism even at the time of Tertullian.[25] According to Harmless, how-ever, the sermons of Augustine provide the first evidence of this distinctive North African ritual; he denies that the treatises of Ter-tullian and Cyprian have this purpose, preferring instead to suggest that these discourses are inspired by the rite, because of references which are made to the eucharist which imply that the hearers knew its shape, and cannot, therefore, be catechumens.[26] This argument presupposes, however, that a *disciplina arcani* was in place in third-century Africa, an assumption which is questionable, to say the

[23]W. Harmless, *Augustine and the Catechumenate* (Collegeville: Liturgical, 1995), 286.

[24]V. Grossi, "Il contesto battesimale dell' oratio dominica nei commenti di Ter-tulliano, Cipriano, Agostino," *Augustinianum*, 20 (1980): 205–220 at 214–217. Both Tertullian and Cyprian refer to the Lord's Prayer as a summary of the Gospel.

[25]So also W. Rordorf, "The Lord's Prayer in the Light of its Liturgical Use in the Early Church," *Studia Liturgica*, 14 (1980–1981): 1–19 at 3.

[26]Harmless, *Augustine and the Catechumenate*, 287 n.169.

least.[27] It is therefore entirely reasonable to see these discourses reflecting the instruction that was given to catechumens in the Lord's Prayer at the last stage of their formation. It is taught at this stage, as the Lord's Prayer is then said by the candidates as they enter the assembly from baptism. Although there is no explicit statement of this in the writings of the third century, Tertullian, at the conclusion of his discourse on baptism, states that the newly baptized should pray to the Father when first they open their hands "in their mother's house" alongside their brothers and as they ascend from the bath of their new birth.[28] Since the newly baptized are here told to pray for the gifts of the Spirit, we may understand that this is common practice, and thus explain the paraphrase of the opening petitions of the Lord's Prayer as given by Marcion: "Father, let your spirit come upon us and purify us,"[29] as well as Perpetua's report that she should ask nothing from her baptism other than endurance in the flesh.[30] The prayer of the newly baptized is still understood as being particularly effective in Africa in the fifth century.[31] In Cyprian's treatise, moreover, there are several allusions that may be best understood as referring to the practice of reciting the Lord's Prayer as the first prayer after baptism:

> A renewed man, reborn and restored to his God by his grace, first of all says "Father," because he is now become a son. . . . Whoever therefore believed in his name is made a child of God, and hence should begin to give thanks and show himself a child of God as he names his Father as God

---

[27]I have argued against the existence of this discipline in "Catechumenate and Contra-Culture."

[28]*On Baptism* 20.

[29]Following F.J. Dölger, "Das erste Gebet der Täuflinge in der Gemeinschaft der Brüder," in *Antike und Christentum* II (Münster: Aschendorff, 1930), 142–155 at 150–151.

[30]*Passion of Perpetua* 3.5.

[31]Thus the report of a miracle at Augustine *City of God* 22.8, and the direction of Quodvultdeus at *Sermon* 7.9.

in heaven. He bears witness also, among the first of his words at his rebirth, that he renounces his earthly and fleshly father . . .

"Our Father," that is of those who believe, of those who have begun to be children of God, sanctified through him and restored by a birth of spiritual grace. (*On the Lord's Prayer* 9–10)

In examining Cyprian's treatise in the light of that already published by Tertullian, we may reasonably suggest that this is an expansion of Tertullian's rather allusive citation of John 1:12 in his discussion of the "Father" of the Lord's Prayer.[32] We may therefore suggest that, even though *Apostolic Constitutions* 7.45.1 is not African, its statement that the Lord's Prayer is said by the newly baptized for the first time is part of a more general understanding of the Lord's Prayer as the prayer of those who are baptized, all of which explains the function of the handing-over of the Lord's Prayer with its accompanying teaching at the late stage of the catechumenate.

We may go on to suggest that this rite explains the production of these treatises; that is, they reflect the instruction that was given at the *traditio orationis*. Whereas this is probable in itself, we should attempt to see what other evidence exists within the discourses for their origin.

Turning first to Tertullian's treatise, we may note Simpson's suggestion that it belongs in the same group as *On Penitence* and *On Baptism*.[33] Tertullian explicitly states in *On Baptism* that he is addressing himself to those in the final stages of preparation for baptism, and although there is no such direct indication in *On Prayer* that this is the audience, it is quite likely that the three belong together by virtue of their origin in the preparation of catechumens.

[32]So Dölger "Erste Gebet," 148.

[33]R. L. Simpson, *The Interpretation of Prayer in the Early Church* (Philadelphia: Westminster, 1965), 20–21.

With regard to Cyprian's work, Simpson suggests that both the manner of the exposition, which breaks the prayer down into its units with comment, and the content of the exposition, which is much occupied with the ethics of Christian living, are appropriate to a catechetical treatise. We may support that by noting that there are several allusions to baptism within the treatise, such as his reference to the prayer made by the newly baptized:

> He bears witness also, among the first of his words at his rebirth, that he renounces his earthly and fleshly father and acknowledges that he has begun to have the Father in heaven as his only father. (9)

> The will of God should be done on earth, that is among those who do not believe, so that those who are earthly from their original birth should begin to be heavenly, being born of water and the spirit. (17)

and

> He wishes that we should remain as we are when we are reborn in our second birth, that those who are children of God should remain in the peace of God. (23)

There are few indicators of an audience in Tertullian's address, and did we not know otherwise of the *traditio orationis* the connection between these works and the preparation of catechumens might not be made. However, as Simpson points out with particular regard to the aptness of the material presented by Cyprian to catechetical address, the collective weight of all these considerations is impressive.[34]

We have established that Tertullian's discourse was given in his capacity as a *senior*, but may assume that Cyprian delivered his

[34]Simpson, *Interpretation*, 59.

address in his capacity as bishop. We may now pause to consider the reason for this change, and may suggest that it comes about as a result of Cyprian's perception that, within his diocese, the bishop is a sole and supreme governor. This receives liturgical expression in the rite of laying on a hand after baptism. Tertullian, in his treatise on baptism, stated that the newly baptized received a laying on of a hand after baptism, which signified the receipt of the Holy Spirit.[35] He states, moreover, that the normal minister of baptism is the bishop,[36] which would mean that the laying on of hands for the reception of the Holy Spirit would normally be received from the bishop, but there is an implication, however, that others may perform the same rite. At Cyprian's time this rite is restricted to the bishop alone,[37] which in turn implies that at this time the bishop, under normal circumstances, would be the sole agent of baptism. As such, each candidate is visibly baptized into the single church, for which reason Cyprian, in his dispute with Rome, is unable to accept that baptism at the hands of anyone not in communion with the bishop has any effect. As the bishop is now the baptizer, we may thus envisage that those from the environs of Carthage would come to the city and to the bishop for baptism. Such a practice is still found at the time of Augustine.[38] Since, however, the bishop is now the agent of baptism and candidates are therefore coming to the city for baptism, it makes sense to see the bishop himself giving the final discourse to the gathered catechumens on the same occasion that they receive their final exorcism.

[35] On Baptism 8.
[36] On Baptism 17.
[37] Letter 69.11.3; 72.1.1.
[38] See Harmless, Augustine and the Catechumenate, 244, who cites the example of Curma, from Tullium, at On the Care to be taken of the Dead 12.15.

THE LITERARY HISTORY OF THE DISCOURSES

Although the genesis of both discourses lies in the instruction on the Lord's Prayer given to catechumens before baptism, in order that they might make that prayer on coming out of the water, Tertullian goes on, after the commentary on the Lord's Prayer, to discuss other matters relating to prayer, both regarding the proper disposition of prayer and various customs and habits relating to the practice of prayer in his community. The shape of the two discourses may be compared thus:

TERTULLIAN	CYPRIAN
	1–3: The Lord's Prayer was given by the Lord, and should be prayed
	4–6: On modesty in approach to prayer (cf. Tertullian 17 and stray comments passim)
	7: Text of the Lord's Prayer
	8: Prayer as corporate
1: The Lord's Prayer as compendium of all prayers	9a: The Lord's Prayer as compendium of all prayers
2–3a: Father in heaven	9b–11: Our Father in heaven
3b: Hallowed be your name	12: Hallowed be your name
4: Let your will be done in heaven and on earth	14–16: Let your will be done in heaven and on earth
5: Let your Kingdom come	13: Let your Kingdom come
6: Give us today our daily bread	18–21: Give us today our daily bread
7: Forgive us our debts . . .	22–24: Forgive us our debts . . .
8: Do not lead us into temptation but deliver us from the evil one	25–26: Do not let us be led into temptation
	27: Deliver us from the evil one
9: Summary of foregoing	28: Summary of foregoing

All the topics with which both Cyprian and Tertullian deal are appropriate matters of instruction for catechumens, but those controversial issues with which Tertullian alone deals do not belong in this context, which makes their inclusion all the more peculiar.

Whereas there seems little logic in the order of the controversial topics with which Tertullian deals, or indeed the connection of the various topics with that of the Lord's Prayer, there are no obvious redactional seams, apart from the introduction of the veiling of virgins, which seems to interrupt the flow and is of inordinate length within the treatise. However, at this point Tertullian has already dealt with various controversial practices, so we cannot claim that these chapters alone are interpolations. Thus we may follow Simpson and Evans in suggesting that the controversial material has been edited into an existing treatise,[39] but that some care has been taken in doing so, and that this is not, therefore, some accident of transmission. As supporting evidence for this suggestion we may note that the controversial chapters are much more finished than those on the Lord's Prayer, which seem to serve more as *aides-memoire* than as completed prose.[40] The revision of material for publication was a practice familiar to Tertullian,[41] and so it should not surprise us that *On Prayer* appears to have undergone such a procedure, and that it has been prepared for publication as a work on prayer, and that the instruction of catechumens (which was in any case oral) is not the purpose of the published work, although such a discourse was employed in the redaction of the present treatise. We may note that Tertullian's treatise on baptism similarly extends rather beyond the information which might reasonably be imparted to catechumens, and that a similar process might have been undergone by that treatise likewise in preparation for publication.

If this is agreed, the next question is the source of the additional material. We may reasonably assume, in view of the acerbic style manifested in these chapters, that this is the work of Tertullian himself, but must ask whether there was a context for their original delivery, or whether they were produced for inclusion in this treatise, and the rationale by which they are included.

---

[39]Simpson, *Interpretation*, 22; Evans, *Tertullian's Tract*, xii.

[40]Simpson, *Interpretation*, 22.

[41]On Tertullian's revision of material see W. Tabbernee "Noiseless Books and Pilfered Manuscripts: Early Christian 'Desk-Top' Publishing in Carthage" at http://divinity.library.vanderbilt.edu/burns/chroma/reading/tabberneebks.html.

However, it is not possible to discern a logic by which a particular group in the African church might be identified as a consistent
opponent, giving rise either to the publication of the work or the
original production of all the polemical material. For whereas the
washing of hands before prayer and the failure to kneel on the Sabbath may indicate that there was a group sympathetic to Judaism in
the African church, the practice of those who abstain from the
pax whilst fasting and from the eucharist whilst keeping a station
would, on the basis of their emphasis on fasting, seem to be the pro-
Montanist group to which Tertullian in time belonged. Those who
sit down after prayer appeal to the work of Hermas, but it is hard on
this basis to identify any one party to which they belong (though
Hermas himself keeps a station[42]).

The impossibility of determining a consistent opponent, the
apparent lack of logic in the inclusion of these chapters, and the
more finished style of these chapters than those on the Lord's Prayer
make it improbable that they were produced solely for inclusion in
the treatise. They therefore had existence prior to the redaction of
the existing treatise.

Given, again, that there is no consistent opponent, the suggestion which seems most probable is that these are judgments given
by Tertullian in his capacity as a *senior* in the Carthaginian church.
Just as one of the functions of this group was the adjudication of
prophecy, and just as Cyprian had cause to consult this group in
making decisions concerning the readmission of various penitents,[43] we may suggest that among the judicial functions of this
group were regulation of the conduct of worship in the community
and evaluation of various controversial practices. We may thus suggest that this is the origin of the various judgments on diverse practices that Tertullian delivers in this work, namely they have come
from Tertullian in his office of *senior*. They are included in a work

[42]Hermas *Similitude* 5.1.1.
[43]*Letter* 38.2.

on prayer that is partly redacted from the address to catechumens, which he gave in that same capacity.

Although it is not possible to define a single opponent in Tertullian's treatise, an overall approach in Tertullian's responses can be discerned. Tertullian's concern is principally that the entire community should be separate from wider society. Thus he rejects the washing of hands and refusal to kneel on the Sabbath as marks of Jewish practice, and the removal of garments and the act of sitting after prayer[44] because these are marks of paganism; Christians are to be absolutely distinct. However, as a distinct community and peculiar people they are to be united in their practice, and so a station is not to disrupt participation in Communion nor fasting to prevent participation in the *pax*.

By contrast to the complex editorial history of Tertullian's treatise, we may suggest that Cyprian's discourse has undergone relatively little editing, and stands as it was first delivered, thus providing us with a closer representation of the material delivered to those preparing for baptism.

The final question which needs to be addressed in considering the literary history of these discourses is that of whether the proximity between Cyprian's and Tertullian's addresses on the Lord's Prayer comes about as a result of Cyprian's direct debt to Tertullian or because of the extent to which both drew on an established tradition of commentary and of the subjects which might be covered in that commentary. Certainly, as we have seen, Cyprian was conscious of Tertullian as master, and had occasion to refer to his works, but equally certainly Cyprian's work is not a direct imitation of that of Tertullian, not least because, as von der Goltz points out, the very text of the prayer which the two give is different.[45] Nonetheless, the

---

[44]Rather than sitting, the prayers should conclude with the *pax*. So, not only *On prayer* 18, but *Passion of Perpetua* 12.6. On the subject as a whole see F. J. Dölger, "Das Niedersitzen nach dem Gebet," in *Antike und Christentum* V (Münster: Aschendorff, 1936), 116–137.

[45]E. von der Goltz, *Das Gebet in der ältesten Christenheit* (Leipzig: Hinrichs,

two treatises are close both in shape and in content. However, given that the works are different, and yet that the shape of Cyprian's work may be discerned behind part of Tertullian's work, whereas Tertullian's treatise would have reached Cyprian in its published and interpolated form, we may state that the structure of the address, namely a general consideration of prayer, followed by a commentary on the Lord's Prayer, and final instructions on times for prayer, was traditional and represented the wider practice of the African church.[46] On the other hand, it is to be noted that Cyprian in particular makes a number of points not made by Tertullian, and in speaking of the unity that is so essential in the body of the baptized seems specifically to be addressing the situation which he met in the period after his return from exile, which leads to the suggestion that the precise contents of the commentary would be left to the speaker. Finally, although the content of the commentary might be left to the discretion of the speaker, it is possible that each individual discourse might be influenced at some points by some tradition of exposition; both, for instance, deal with the Lord's instructions on praying in secret, both quote from the sixth chapter of John in dealing with the petition for daily bread whilst expressing concern lest any find themselves separated from the "daily bread," both deal with the parable of the unforgiving slave in dealing with the petition to be forgiven as we forgive others. Other points of contact noted by Simpson are the interpretation of the petition for the coming of the Kingdom as applying to the individual Christian within the church and the combination of literal and spiritual in the interpretation of "bread."[47]

In these two discourses we therefore hear not only the instruction of catechumens in the prayer of the faithful, but also the

1901), 282. See, however, our comment in the appendix below on the possibility that Tertullian had deliberately inverted the order of the prayer.

[46]Similarly von der Goltz, *Gebet*, 284 n. 1, though, as G. F. Diercks, *De Oratione: critische Unitgave met prolegomena, Vertaling en philologisch-exegetisch-liturgische Commentaar* (Bussum: Paul Brand, 1947), LXVIII n. 10, points out, von der Goltz underestimates the extent of Cyprian's debt to Tertullian.

[47]Simpson, *Interpretation*, 27.

preoccupations and concerns of Tertullian the *senior* and Cyprian the bishop, each in their way concerned with the regulation of a community which had set itself outside the normal conventions of life in third-century Africa.

APPENDIX I: THE LITURGICAL SETTING OF THE PRACTICES REGULATED BY TERTULLIAN

Tertullian takes issue with a number of practices surrounding gatherings of Christians. At issue is whether these are gatherings for prayer at the times described by himself and by Cyprian, as times at which prayer should be offered, gatherings for the eucharist,[48] or other occasions.

The nineteenth chapter is clearly concerned with practice at the eucharist, as the issue concerns those who do not receive communion for fear of breaking their fast. This implies that the station days were marked by the celebration of the eucharist, even though these stations, whilst widely observed, were not binding upon Christians. At the time of Cyprian there was, in Carthage at least, a daily celebration of the eucharist;[49] Tertullian, however, implies that the custom of receiving communion daily at home was also known in Carthage, which implies that a daily celebration was not necessarily the norm at that time,[50] and we may therefore suggest that the eucharist was celebrated to mark the stational day.

Although this chapter is therefore concerned with the eucharist, this need not mean that the same applies to the other chapters, as these are each individual judgments given on various occasions, and applying therefore to different aspects of Christian life in Carthage. Each chapter should therefore be read separately.[51]

[48]As Evans, *Tertullian's Tract*, assumes.
[49]*Letter* 54.3; 56.1.
[50]In agreement with C. W. Dugmore, *The Influence of the Synagogue upon the Divine Office*, 2nd ed. (Westminster: Faith Press, 1964), 55, on the basis of *To His Wife* 2.5.
[51]Cf. Jorg Christian Salzmann, *Lehren und Ermahnen: zur Geschichte des*

In the eighteenth chapter we hear that there are those who abstain from the kiss of peace as the seal of the prayer when they are fasting. Although it is not clear what prayer is meant, the following are possible:

1) That the prayer is the intercession, and that the *pax* takes place in the position known to Justin,[52] namely before the offering of the gifts. Against this, however, is the evidence which suggests that this was never the position of the *pax* in Africa, but rather that the *pax* took place immediately before Communion.[53]
2) That the eucharistic canon is meant. Against this is the fact that the Lord's Prayer, as noted above, intervenes between the canon and the *pax*.
3) The only remaining possibility is therefore that the Lord's Prayer itself is meant. But this need not point to an eucharistic context, as the Lord's Prayer might conceivably be said at other gatherings, such as gatherings for instruction which, in Rome in any event, concluded with the peace.

Two arguments might point to an eucharistic context. First, when Tertullian states that the *pax* is omitted when the whole community is fasting, this points us to the omission of the *pax* in the Roman rite on Good Friday. This rite, albeit without communion, maintains a number of aspects pointing to the primitive liturgy, such as the preservation of solemn prayers that have otherwise dropped out of the rite. However, the Roman Good Friday rite was a rite at which the eucharist was not celebrated, and it is possible that the same shape would have been given to a non-eucharistic synaxis. Second, it might be suggested that the Lord's Prayer would not be

christlichen Wortgottesdienstes in der ersten drei Jahrhunderten, WUNT 2, Reihe 59 (Tübingen: Mohr, 1994), 403, who assumes that chapter 18 refers to the eucharist because that is the referent of chapter 19.

[52]Described at *First Apology* 65. This position is adopted by Evans, *Tertullian's Tract,* 56 and Salzmann, *Lehren und Ermahnen,* 426.

[53]According to Augustine *Sermon* 149.16, 227.

said at a gathering for instruction principally concerned with the direction of catechumens, since the prayer was the sole property of the baptized. The objection to the second suggestion may be raised that catechumens and faithful might pray separately after instruction,[54] and that this separation would not prevent the saying of the Lord's Prayer by the faithful. It is possible that the baptized also attended for instruction.

Apart from gatherings for instruction or for eucharist, it is possible that gatherings took place for prayer, though there is not a great deal which supports this, even though Dugmore, on the basis of the statement of Cyprian that prayer should be "common and collective,"[55] assumes that this refers to daily gatherings for prayer alone.[56] According to Cyprian the duty of the clergy is to be devoted to the sacrifices and prayers,[57] for which reason they were to keep aloof from worldly responsibilities. It would not be possible, however, for all Christians to be kept so aloof, and so we may suggest that gathering for prayer at the hours was uncommon. However, a gathering for instruction and prayer early in the morning, like that described in *Apostolic Tradition*, is conceivable. This occasion is hinted at in the peroration of Tertullian's treatise. As has been noted, at the time of Cyprian the eucharist was offered daily, but it is possible that this was a development out of gatherings for instruction and prayer. Finally, this suggestion may gain support from the statement of Tertullian at *On the Apparel of Women* 2.11, who describes the occasions on which Christian women might be out, noting among them either the offering of the sacrifice or the sharing of the word of God.[58]

---

[54]So not only in Africa (*Prescription against Heretics* 41) but also in Rome (Hippolytus *Apostolic Tradition* 18.1).

[55]*On the Lord's Prayer* 8.

[56]Dugmore, *Influence*, 49–50. Cf. P. F. Bradshaw, *Daily Prayer in the Early Church* (London: SPCK, 1981), 65: "There is nothing in the evidence . . . which would lead to the conclusion that the times of daily prayer were celebrated corporately in the early church, and much that would suggest the opposite . . ."

[57]*Letter* 1.1.

[58]"Aut sacrificium offertur aut dei sermo administratur."

There is also reference to the sealing of the prayer in chapter six-
teen, as Tertullian inveighs against those who sit down at this point,
but there is no indication in this chapter of the occasion which is
meant. Nonetheless, given that the *pax* is meant as the true sealing
of prayer, and that this concludes prayer but does not conclude the
eucharist, we may reasonably see this applying to the conclusion of
a gathering for instruction, which concluded with prayer. The fact
that the pagan custom to which Tertullian refers as being comparable is generally domestic does not affect the issue, as the gathering
took place in a household-church. Moreover, the polemic against
those who refuse to kneel on the Sabbath (in the twenty-third chapter) may again point to a gathering for instruction rather than for
eucharist for, although later centuries record the Sabbath as an occasion on which the eucharist might be offered, the more ancient tradition, deriving from Judaism, is one which sets the Sabbath aside as
a day for study. The day might end with a celebration, and this celebration, which was originally a celebration associated with the Sunday, which according to Jewish reckoning began at the eve of
Sabbath, might in time become associated with the Sabbath as the
origin of the gathering on Saturday evening is forgotten. But this is
not the original purpose of this day, and the evidence for the celebration of the eucharist on the Sabbath is relatively late, whereas
gathering for instruction on this day is attested early. Unfortunately,
none of this evidence is African, though one might expect the practice of African Christians to cohere at this point with that of Christians elsewhere. Two strands of evidence support this supposition.
First, the outlook of those opposed by Tertullian, who are attempt-
ing to coalesce Sabbath and Sunday, is indicative of the change
within Judaism which was taking place at the time, which was to
turn the Sabbath into a day of celebration and rejoicing rather than
study.[59] This indicates that the original purpose of the Sabbath gatherings in Africa is under attack. Second, at the time of Augustine, the

[59]For a discussion of this point and full references see my *Vita Polycarpi: An
Anonymous Vita from Third-Century Smyrna* (Sydney: St Paul's, 2002), 55–58, 61–67.

traditio and *redditio symboli* were occasions that took place on a Saturday. It is possible that this is a survival from the practice of teaching on the Sabbath.

No clue is left us regarding the occasion of the other issues of controversy with which Tertullian deals, though the discussion of washing hands in the thirteenth chapter may well apply to private prayer as there is a discussion of this practice, relating to private prayer, in *Apostolic Tradition* 41.

Thus, in conclusion, we may suggest that Tertullian, as *senior*, is seeking to regulate both gatherings for the eucharist and gatherings for instruction early in the morning. There were no gatherings for prayer at regular hours apart, perhaps, from prayer at the ninth hour on station days. Since Tertullian describes a gathering for food distinct from celebrations at the eucharist, known as the *agapē*,[60] it is possible that this took place at the ninth hour, and marked the public breaking of the fast at the hour at which it was usual to take a main meal. Tertullian implies that the *agapē* took place before nightfall, as lamps are only brought in halfway through the meal. The Marcionites knew a meal of agapic character called the *cena pura* (pure supper),[61] derived from Jewish practice, which took place on Friday evenings, being the first evening of the Sabbath (which ran from nightfall) and it is possible that the *agapē* of Tertullian's Africa derived from the same origin. No regulation of this meal, however, can be discerned in the instructions contained in *On Prayer*.

Appendix II: The Hours of Prayer in Third-Century Africa

The pattern of prayer which both Tertullian and Cyprian promote, namely prayer in the morning and evening, three times in the course

---

[60] *Apology* 39.

[61] See on the *cena pura* my "Bread, Fish, Water and Wine: The Marcionite Menu and the Maintenance of Purity" in G. May and K. Greschat, eds., *Marcion und seine kirchengeschichtliche Wirkung*, TU 150 (Berlin: de Gruyter, 2002), 207–220.

of the day, and at midnight, differs from that of Origen, but is the same as that of the *Apostolic Tradition*. The section of *Apostolic Tradition* that presents the timetable is, as I have argued elsewhere, one of the later parts of that composite document and is probably contemporary with Cyprian. It is possible that it originated in Africa and travelled thence to Rome.

The origin of this timetable is much debated. I have suggested, building on the work of Bradshaw, that it is actually a fusion of two separate patterns of prayer, both derived from Judaism.[62] One pattern prescribed prayer in the morning, in the afternoon, and in the evening, whereas the other prescribed prayer at dawn, midday, dusk, and midnight (the pattern, incidentally, known to Origen). It is even possible that this fusion took place in Africa, though the manner in which Tertullian groups the three hours of the day together, separately from morning and evening, and separately again from prayer at midnight, suggests that the pattern was already traditional when Tertullian wrote, and that its origin was therefore forgotten.

APPENDIX III: THE DIFFERING TEXTS OF THE LORD'S PRAYER

The following table, based on those supplied by Réveillaud and Diercks,[63] illustrates the differing texts of the prayer to be found in Africa. Beyond those which may readily be noticed there are a number of subtle differences that cannot be conveyed in translation. Nonetheless it is noteworthy that there are such differences, in that this shows that it is improbable that the prayer was recited publicly or in common, for at that point the differences between versions would emerge.

---

[62]"Prayer Five Times in the Day and at Midnight: Two Apostolic Customs!" *Studia Liturgica*, 33 (2003): 1–19; the article is indebted to the discussion of Bradshaw, *Daily Prayer*.

[63]Réveillaud, *L'Oraison dominicale*, 168–169; Diercks, *De oratione* XLVI–XLVII.

TERTULLIAN[64]	CYPRIAN	AFRICAN BIBLE	AUGUSTINE
Father, you who are in the heavens,	Our Father, you who are in the heavens,	Our Father, you who are in the heavens,	Our Father, you who are in the heavens,
let your name be hallowed,	let your name be hallowed,	let your name be hallowed,	let your name be hallowed,
	let your Kingdom come,	may your Kingdom come,	let your Kingdom come,
let your will be done in the heavens and on the earth, may your Kingdom come.	let your will be done in heaven and on earth.	let your will be done in heaven and on earth.	let your will be done, just as in heaven, also on earth.
Give us this day our daily bread,	Give us this day our daily bread,	Give us this day our daily bread,	Give us this day our daily bread,
pardon us our debts	and pardon our debts	and pardon us our debts	and pardon us our debts
as we too pardon our debtors,	just as we pardon our debtors,	just as we pardon our debtors,	just as we pardon our debtors,
do not lead us into temptation,	and do not allow us to be led into temptation,	and never allow us to be led into temptation,	and do not allow us to be borne into temptation,
but remove us from the evil one.	but set us free from the evil one.	but set us free from the evil one. Since the power is yours in the ages of the ages.	but set us free from the evil one.

[64]The order of exposition in Tertullian's treatise is followed here, in which the usual order of the petitions for the coming of the Kingdom and for the performance of God's will are inverted. There is some doubt as to whether that was the order in which Tertullian knew the prayer, for as Diercks (*De Oratione*, 103–104) points out, Tertullian uses the first person singular in introducing these petitions, whereas elsewhere he attributes the order of each petition to the Lord, which implies that he had made the inversion himself. Diercks suggests that his rationale is to enable the commentary to climax in a petition for the performance of God's will in ourselves. We might further note that the Marcionite interpretation of the Kingdom as the gift of the Holy Spirit is thereby implicitly negated, as it is separated from the hallowing of the name of God.

Tertullian: *On Prayer*

1

The Spirit of God and the Word of God and the reason of God, the
Word of reason and the reason of the Word,[1] both of which are
spirit,[2] namely Jesus Christ our Lord, marked out for his new disciples of the new covenant a new form of prayer. It was fitting that, in
this instance likewise, new wine should be stored in new bottles and
a new patch be stitched to a new garment (Mt 9.17 and par.). Whatever was of the old has either been transformed, as has circumcision,
or else completed, as was the remainder of the law, or fulfilled, as
prophecy has been, or perfected, as is faith itself. As the Gospel has
been introduced as the completion of everything of antiquity, the
new grace of God has renewed all things from fleshly being into spiritual being. In it our Lord Jesus Christ is recognized as the Spirit of
God and the Word of God and the reason of God. He is spirit in view
of his power, Word in view of his teaching, and reason because he
came among us. Thus the prayer which is instituted by Christ is
made up of three parts: out of word, by which it is spoken, out of
spirit, by which it is powerful, out of reason, in that it reconciles.

John taught his disciples to pray (Lk 11.1); but everything that
was of John was laid down in advance of Christ, until he himself
should increase (just as John foretold that he should increase, and
that he should himself decrease [Jn 3.30]), and the whole work of the

---

[1]"Word" and "reason" are both possible translations of the Greek *logos*. In this
chapter Tertullian uses the term "reason" to signify not an attribute of God alone, but
also God's reason in acting, namely salvation.

[2]Tertullian, in common with other Christians of his age, does not carefully dis-
tinguish the Holy Spirit from the spirit that is the nature of God, although in later
works, in particular his work *Against Praxeas*, we have the beginnings of a distinction.

forerunner should pass over, with the Spirit, to the Lord. Therefore the words in which John taught them to pray are not extant, because earthly things should yield to heavenly. "Whoever is of the earth," he says, "speaks earthly things, and whoever is present from the heavens speaks of those things which he has seen" (Jn 3.31–32). And whatever is heavenly is of the Lord Christ, as is this rule of prayer likewise.

Therefore let us consider, blessed ones, his heavenly wisdom, firstly regarding his instruction to pray in secret (Mt 6.6), by which he both demands that a person believe, in that he should be confident in the ability of almighty God to hear and to see in houses, and indeed in a hidden chamber, and desires a proportionate faith, that he should trust him who is everywhere to hear and to see, and should offer his devotion to him alone. There is further wisdom in the command which follows, which likewise pertains to the measure of faith and the proportion of faith, that we should not consider going to God, of whose regard for those who are his own we are assured, with an army of words (Mt 6.7–8). Yet that brevity rests upon the foundation of a great and blessed understanding, and as much as it is restricted in words, it is comprehensive in meaning. Herein is a third level of wisdom; for not only are all the occasions of prayer included, whether divine worship or human petition, but the whole discourse of the Lord is included, the whole record of his instruction, so that, without exaggeration, a summary of the whole Gospel is to be found in the prayer.

2

It begins with bearing witness to God and with the reward of faith when we say:[3] "Father, you who are in the heavens."

For we are praying to God and confessing the faith of which this mode of address is an indication. It is written: "To those who believe in him, he gave power to be called children of God" (Jn 1.12). For that

[3]For a discussion of the translation of this phrase, see R. L. Simpson, *The Interpretation of Prayer in the Early Church* (Philadelphia: Westminster, 1965), 46.

matter the Lord most frequently proclaimed to us that God is Father, indeed, he also demanded that we should call nobody "father" on earth, except him whom we have in heaven (Mt 23.9). Therefore, when we pray in this way, we are being obedient to that direction; happy are they who acknowledge the Father! It is on these grounds that Israel is reproached, because the Spirit calls heaven and earth to bear witness as he says: "I have begotten sons and they have not acknowledged me" (Is 1.2).

However, when we say "Father" we are also naming God in a form of address which demonstrates both devotion and power.[4] Moreover the Son is invoked in the Father, for he says: "I and the Father are one" (Jn 10.30). Nor is the mother, the church, neglected, since the mother is found within the Father and the Son, for the name of Father and Son find their meaning in her.[5] Therefore under one term and with one name we honor God along with those who are his, both recalling God's commandment and scorning those who have forgotten the Father.

3

The name of God the Father had been revealed to nobody. Even Moses, who had asked it of God himself, heard of a different name (Ex 3.14–15). But to us it is revealed in the Son, for now we know that Son is the new name of the Father. "I have come," he said, "in the name of the Father" (Jn 5.43). And again: "Father, glorify your name" (Jn 12.28). And, more openly: "I have made your name known to people" (Jn 17.6). It is that name whose hallowing we beseech, not because it is fitting for people to give God our good wishes, as though there were another from whom it might be possible that

---

[4]*Pietas* (here translated "devotion," as the term carries connotations both of love and obedience), and *potestas* (power) are the marks of a father in a Roman family.

[5]Compare Tertullian's statement at *On Baptism* 6, which derives from the article of faith in the church in the African version of the creed. Cyprian likewise recognizes the church as the mother of the believer. So, in *On Unity* 6, he states: "One cannot have God as a Father without having the church as a mother."

such wishes be received, or as though he might be in trouble did we not wish him well; obviously it is fitting that God should be blessed in every place and time with a view to the fitting remembrance of his gifts from every person. But this clause nonetheless serves the purpose of speaking well. Besides, when is the name of God not of itself both holy and hallowed, since of himself he hallows others, to whom the attendant angels do not cease to say: "Holy, holy, holy."[6] Therefore we likewise who, should we prove worthy, are to put on angelic vesture,[7] are here already learning that heavenly song to God and that task of future glory. This much concerns the glory of God.

Besides this, as regarding our own request, when we say: "Let your name be hallowed," we ask that it be hallowed among us who are in him and, at the same time, in others whom the grace of God still awaits, so that we should be obedient to the command to pray for all, even for our enemies (Mt 5.44). Consequently, as a result of this terse expression, we do not say "Let it be hallowed in us," but manage to say: "in all people."

4

Following this pattern we subjoin: "Let your will be done in the heavens and on the earth."

We are asking that his will be done in all people and not, because somebody is resisting the will of God, out of a need to pray that he

[6]This is not necessarily a reference to the liturgical singing of this hymn, for the hymn is found sung in Greek, rather than Latin, at *The Passion of Perpetua and Felicity* 4.2, a passage which seems to reflect the liturgy of the African church at the time of Tertullian.

[7]The understanding of Tertullian's meaning which leads to the translation of this phrase is based on *On the Resurrection of the Flesh* 36: "they shall be like angels, neither marrying nor dying, but having passed on into an angelic state through putting on incorruption, altered through our resurrected material." In other words, the resurrection body is made of a similar substance to that of which the angels are made, and on this basis Christians in general, and those preparing for baptism in particular, are "angel-candidates." The image is suggested both by the idea of putting on immortality and the clothing in white which was part of the baptismal ritual in Tertullian's Africa.

be successful in implementing it. For, by a figurative interpretation of flesh and spirit, the heaven and the earth indicate ourselves. Even were this clause to be understood superficially the meaning of the petition would be the same: that the will of God be done among us on earth in order that it might occur in heaven likewise. For what would God wish other than that we should act in accordance with his direction? We ask therefore that the substance and ability of his will should assist us, so that we should be saved both in heaven and on the earth, because the sum total of his will is the salvation of those whom he has adopted. And that same will of God is that which the Lord revealed to us in his proclamation and in his labors and in his suffering. For if he himself declared that he did not do his own will but that of his Father (Jn 6.3–39), undoubtedly those things he did were the will of the Father. Thus we are now challenged by these as being exemplary, that we should likewise proclaim and labor and suffer even to death; our ability to do these things is through the will of God.

At the same time, when we say, "Let your will be done," we wish ourselves well because there is nothing of evil in the will of God, even if something of this be imposed on us in accordance with our deserving. Thus, even as we say this phrase, we forewarn ourselves of the need for endurance. The Lord likewise, when he desired to demonstrate in his own flesh the weakness of the flesh through the suffering of the passion, said: "Father, take away this cup." And, recollecting himself: "Nonetheless, let not my will but yours be done" (Mt 26.39 and par.). He was himself the will and the power of the Father, and yet, in order to show the endurance that is due, he abandoned himself to the Father's will.

5

"May your Kingdom come" likewise pertains to the same matter as "let your will be done," namely among ourselves.

For when is God, in whose hand is the heart of all kings (Prov 21.1), not the king? But whatever we choose we suppose to be his, and attribute to him whatever we hope for from him. Therefore, if the open manifestation of the Lord's Kingdom pertains to the will of God and to our expectation, how could anyone ask for an extension of this world, when the Kingdom of God, for whose coming we pray, is directed toward the consummation of this world. We should seek to reign the sooner and not to be enslaved the longer. Even if nothing were laid down in the prayer regarding asking for the coming of the Kingdom we should ourselves have expressed such an appeal while hurrying to the completion of our hope. The souls of the martyrs beneath the altar are crying out to the Lord: "How long, O Lord? Will you not avenge our blood on the inhabitants of the earth?" (Rev 6.10); for their vengeance is instigated at the end of the age. So let your Kingdom come, Lord, all the more speedily, the desire of Christians, the confounding of the gentiles, the joy of angels, for which we are afflicted, for which we pray all the more fervently.[8]

6

But how gracefully did divine wisdom draw up the order of the prayer that, after petitions for the name of God, the will of God and the Kingdom of God, it should also provide a place for earthly needs. For the Lord declared: "Seek first the Kingdom, and then all these things will be added to you" (Mt 6.33).

Nonetheless, we should understand "Give us this day our daily bread" better in a spiritual sense. For Christ is our bread, because Christ is life and bread is life. "I am," he said, "The bread of life." And a little earlier, "The bread is the word of the living God who came down from the heavens" (Jn 6.48). Then, because his body is accounted bread: "This is my body" (Mt 26.26 and par.; 1 Cor 11.24). Therefore, when we ask for our daily bread, we are asking that we should perpetually be in Christ and that we should not be separated from his body.

[8] It is possible, given the similar wording at Cyprian *On the Lord's Prayer* 35, that this is an allusion to an actual prayer in use at Carthage.

Although that clause is open to a carnal interpretation, it may, with great devotion, be understood to apply to spiritual practice. For he commands us to ask for the bread which is all that the faithful require, whereas the gentiles seek after other things. Thus he both enforces our learning with illustrations and rehearses it in parables as he says: "Would a father take away bread from his children and hand it over to dogs" (Mt 15.26). And again: "Would he hand his son a stone when he asks for bread?" (Mt 7.9) He shows what children anticipate from a father, since the man who knocked at night was knocking for bread. He adds, rightly: "Give it today," as he had already laid down that we should "Take no thought for what you should eat tomorrow" (Mt 6.34). Along similar lines he had already provided the parable of that man who, in view of the abundance of his produce, considered the extension of his barns and a lengthy period of security, when he would die that very night (Lk 12.16–21).

7

It is consonant then that, having observed the liberality of God, we should also beseech his mercy. For what will food profit us if its reason is to render us a bull for sacrifice? The Lord knew that he alone was without wrong, so he taught us to pray: "Pardon us our debts."

A confession is a request for pardon, because whoever asks pardon confesses a wrongdoing.[9] So it is shown that penitence is acceptable to God, because he desires this, rather than the death of a sinner (cf. Ezek 8.23). A debt, in Scripture, is an image of a wrongdoing, because wrongdoing always owes a debt to judgment and is avenged by it; neither does it avoid the justice of restitution unless restitution be given, just as the master remitted the debt of his servant. For the lesson of the entire parable points this out. Our profession that we too "pardon our debtors" is consonant with the fact that the same

---

[9]Tertullian refers to the practice of confession before the church, by which a person might be put into an intermediate state of being a penitent, neither within the church nor entirely without. See his description of the process at *On Penitence* 9.

servant, who was set free by his master but would in turn not spare his debtor, was on this account brought before his master and sent to torture until he should pay the very last cent (Mt 18.23–26), that is the very slightest wrongdoing. And elsewhere, in keeping with this clause of the prayer, he says: "Forgive and it will be forgiven you" (Lk 6.37). And when Peter asked him whether he should forgive his brother seventy times he said "Rather, seventy times seven" (Mt 18.21). Thus he cast the law in better form, because in Genesis vengeance was reckoned seven times in the case of Cain, and seventy times seven in that of Lamech (Gen 4.24).

8

To complete this most succinct prayer he added: "Do not lead us into temptation." That is, do not allow us so to be led by the one that tempts.

This is laid down so that we should not only request the forgiveness of wrongdoing but that we should avoid it entirely. Far be it that the Lord should seem to tempt, as though he were either ignorant of the faith of each of us, or sought to dethrone it, for weakness and malice are of the devil. For he did not order even Abraham to make a sacrifice of his son for the sake of putting his faith to the test but of demonstrating it (Gen 22.1), so that he might provide an example of the instruction which he would in time lay down, that one should not hold even one's children more precious than God (Mt 10.37). He was himself tested by the devil, so demonstrating who the leader and worker of temptation is.

This understanding he clarifies in what follows, as he says: "Pray that you be not put to the test" (Mt 26.41 and par.). In fact, they were tempted into forsaking the Lord because they devoted themselves to sleep, rather than to prayer. Therefore, the conclusion of the prayer corresponds to and interprets the meaning of, "Do not lead us into temptation." For it says: "But remove us from the evil one."[10]

[10]Note the interpretation of these clauses in *On Flight* 2.5, in which Tertullian

9

How many are the statements of the prophets, gospels, and apostles, the words of the Lord, parables, illustrations, instructions, touched on in the pithiness of a very few words, and how many the duties performed on one occasion! We honor God in "Father," witness to the faith in "name," offer obedience in "will," remember our hope in "Kingdom," seek life in "bread," confess our debts in "pardon," show concern for temptation in the request for safekeeping. Why wonder at this? God alone could teach us the manner in which he would have us pray. Therefore, the practice of prayer is laid down by him, and when it was brought forth from the divine mouth it was animated by his spirit. By its own special right it thus goes up to heaven, commending to the Father the things the Son has taught.

10

However, since the Lord, foreseeing all human necessities (Mt 6.8), says elsewhere, after the instruction concerning praying had been delivered, "Ask, and you will receive" (Jn 16.24; cf. Mt 7.7), and since there are things which might be asked according to individual circumstances, we have the right to construct a secondary top-story of pleas for additional desires on the foundation, as it were, of our rehearsal of the proper and normal prayer. Yet we must be mindful of his directions, since our distance from his directions is our distance from the ears of God.

11

By mindfulness of the instructions is the way to heaven paved for prayers. And the chief of them is that we should not go up to the altar of God before resolving whatever there might be of offense or

recognizes that there is no greater test than persecution, but that this is part of God's will, whereas we might be preserved from Satan in persecution.

discord contracted with the brothers (Mt 5.23–24). For how can one approach the peace of God without peace, how seek the remission of debts whilst retaining them? How shall one who is angry with his brother placate the Father, when all anger is forbidden us from the beginning? For even Joseph, when he sent his brothers to fetch their father, said: "And do not grow angry on the way" (Gen 45.24). His advice was meant for us, that we should not travel in anger on the way made up of prayer toward the Father, for elsewhere "way" denotes the practice which is ours. Consequently the Lord, in expanding and clarifying the law, equates anger toward a brother with homicide (Mt 5.22–23). He will not even allow the expression of an angry word. The apostle warns us not to be angry beyond sunset (Eph 4.26), but how rash it is either to spend a day without prayer whilst delaying the satisfaction due to a brother, or to waste prayer by continuing in anger.

12

The intent of prayer should be free not from anger alone but from all manner of perturbation of the soul, as it should be sent forth from the same sort of spirit as that to which it is sent. For a polluted spirit cannot be known by a holy spirit, any more than a saddened spirit may be known by a gladdened spirit, nor a shackled spirit by one that is free. Nobody opens his door to a foe, nor admits anyone except his peer.

13

Moreover what reason is there for going to prayer with hands which are washed but a spirit which is filthy, when the hands themselves are in need of spiritual cleanliness so that they may be lifted up pure of fraud, murder, violence, sorcery, idolatry, and the other stains which originate in the spirit but which are put into effect through the hands?[11] For this is true cleanliness, not that with which the majority is superstitiously concerned, namely rinsing in water even when they have come from bathing their entire body.[12] When I asked searchingly about this and demanded the reason, I found it to be a recollection of Pilate. He washed his hands when he delivered up the Lord (Mt 27.24). We venerate the Lord, we do not betray him. It is better that we should not wash hands and so to show ourselves to be the reverse of this pattern, unless we should need to wash, being aware of impurity caused by human circumstances. Otherwise, the hands that, along with the whole body, have been washed in Christ once for all, are clean enough.

14

Though Israel wash in all its members every day, yet is he never clean. His hands are always undeniably unclean, ever encrusted with the blood of the prophets and of the Lord himself. Hereditary criminals, aware of their ancestral guilt, they dare not lift them up to the Lord lest some Isaiah should cry out, lest Christ should shrink from them. But we do not simply lift them up but spread them out in imitation of the passion of the Lord, so confessing Christ as we pray.[13]

15

But since we have touched upon one matter of empty expression it will not be irksome to observe other practices likewise, which are reasonably to be discredited as vanity, since not one of them is

---

[11]To this list of sins, cf. those of *Against Marcion* 4.9 and *On Shame* 19.

[12]The practice of washing hands before prayer is known in Judaism, and in early Christianity. Hippolytus *On the Apostolic Tradition* 41 prescribes the washing of hands before prayer, and is glossed in a manner which seems to oppose the practice on similar grounds to those stated here by Tertullian, namely those whose entire body has been washed (in baptism) have no need of further cleansing.

[13]The offering of prayer with hands lifted up and stretched out is the normal posture for Christian prayer in the early centuries.

authorized by any injunction, whether dominical or apostolic. Things of this nature are to be considered not religion but superstition, they are affected and forced, are not reasonable service but fussiness, and should surely be suppressed, if only because they put us on a level with the gentiles. For it is the practice of some of them to make their prayer with their coats removed. It is thus that the gentiles attend their idols. But if this were the right thing to do, surely the apostles would have included it when they taught on the manner of prayer, unless some might think that Paul left his cloak behind with Carpus (2 Tim 4.13) when he was praying! Perhaps God might not hear those with their coats on, God who listened to the saints in the furnace of the Babylonian king when they prayed in their pantaloons and their hats (Dan 3.21)!

16

And again, there are those whose custom is to sit down when the prayer is sealed. I perceive no reason, except one which children might offer. What is it? If Hermas, whose writing is called *The Shepherd*, or something like that,[14] had not sat upon his bed when his prayer was finished but had done something else, would we claim that this too should be made an observance. Surely not. For he simply and unreflectively says: "When I had prayed and sat down on the bed." He says this simply as part of the story, and not as an instance of discipline. Otherwise we would only be able to pray in a place where there was a bed, and it would make it contrary to Scripture if anyone sat on a chair or a bench.[15] Moreover, since the gentiles likewise, when they have worshipped their little idols, sit down again,[16]

[14]Early in the third century a clear and agreed scriptural canon had yet to emerge and the *Shepherd* of Hermas was in some parts of the Christian world equated with Scripture. Tertullian is less than convinced of this claim and is somewhat dismissive of the book at *On Shame* 20. The citation below is from Hermas *Vision* 5.1, but it is probable that Hermas means that he receives a vision *whilst* in bed.

[15]The chair was the place of the bishop, a bench probably the seat of the presbyters, but also possibly of the *seniores* (on whom see the introduction).

[16]The practice of sitting down after prayer in non-Christian Africa is described

all the more should this practice, used in idol worship, be reprimanded among us. To this is to be added the crime of disrespect, which even the gentiles, had they any understanding, would appreciate. Since it is disrespectful to sit down in the presence of, and in spite of the presence of, one who is greatly to be revered and esteemed, how much more is it irreligious to act in such a way when in the sight of the living God, whilst the angel of prayer is still standing by? Or are we protesting to God because prayer has tired us out!

17

All the more we shall commend our prayers to God if we worship with restraint and humility, not even raising our hands too high, but lifting them up temperately and soberly, not presumptuously lifting up our countenance.

For the tax collector, whose countenance and prayer alike were humbled and crestfallen, went away justified, though the insolent pharisee did not (Lk 18.14). So it is fitting that the tones of our voice be subdued; if we are heard in proportion to the noise we make we should need additional lungs! But God is a listener not to the voice but to the heart, as this is what he regards (Heb 4.12). The demon of the Pythian oracle says: "I understand him when he is silent, and I listen when he does not speak."[17] Do God's ears listen out for a noise? How then could the prayer of Jonah come up to heaven from the bottom of the belly of the whale, through the entrails of such a huge beast, from the depths of such a great mass of sea (Jon 2.1)? What more reward will be gained by those who worship too vociferously, except that of distracting those nearby? Indeed, by publishing their petitions what are they doing other than praying in public places?

in Apuleius *Florida* 1.1; Tertullian is referring to the domestic practice of worshipping at home. This does not, however, mean that private prayer is intended (contra G. F. Diercks, *De Oratione: critische Unitgave met prolegomena, Vertaling en philologisch-exegetisch-liturgische Commentaar* [Bussum: Paul Brand, 1947], 160–5).

[17]Cited by Herodotus *Histories* 1.47. Tertullian cites other oracles from this chapter of Herodotus in discussing the oracles at *Apology* 22.

18

And now another custom has become established. Those who are fasting, having joined in prayer with the brothers, withdraw from the kiss of peace, which is the seal of prayer.

When, however, should peace more properly be exchanged than when prayer ascends with the additional commendation of this good work? In this way those who have broken their fast may share in that work of ours, as their brothers lend something of their peace. How can prayer be complete when it is divorced from the holy kiss? Does the peace hinder anyone in doing the work of the Lord? What sort of sacrifice is that from which one departs without making peace? Whatever the reason may be, it will not be more important than the observance of the direction by which we are ordered to hide our fasting (Mt 6.16–18), whereas should we abstain from the kiss, it is known that we are fasting. Although, if there is some reason, you might, perhaps, postpone the kiss and yet not be guilty of breaking this direction, should you be at home, among those from whom it is altogether impossible to conceal your fasting. Anywhere else, where you are in a position to disguise your good work, you must be mindful of the direction. Thus you will do justice to the ruling in public and to the custom at home. So on the day of Pascha, when there is a collective and, as it were, public obligation to fast, we rightly put aside the kiss, being unconcerned to conceal an activity in which all participate.

19

Likewise concerning the station days.[18] A number think that they should not participate in the prayers of the sacrifices, because the

[18]Station days, days spent in fasting, were kept, according to Tertullian, *On Fasting* 2.14, on Wednesday and Friday, and concluded at the ninth hour, which was the usual time for a main meal. This practice is alluded to in the *Martyrdom of Fructuosus* 9, where Fructuosus refuses a drugged drink as it is not yet time to breach the station, and so he concludes the station in Heaven. The party of the New Prophecy wished to extend the station beyond this hour (*On Fasting* 10), though this need not mean that the party of the New Prophecy are those concerned with the breach of their stational

station would be breached by receiving the body of the Lord. So, does the eucharist cancel a devout service to God? Or does it bind us the more to God? Would your station not be more dignified if you have stood at the altar of God? By receiving the body of the Lord, and reserving it, both the participation in the sacrifice and the performance of your duty are maintained.[19] If the term "station" takes its name from the military model (for we are the army of God) then neither joy nor sorrow falling upon a camp releases the soldiers from their station.[20] For joy will cause them to do their duty more cheerfully, and sorrow more carefully.

20

Concerning clothing, at least that of women, the variety of usage has caused me, a man of less than no account, presumptuously to write a treatise after the manner of the most holy apostle,[21] though perhaps it is not presumptuous if my treatment follows that of the

fast by reception of the eucharist, which would happen early in the morning.

[19]In other words, Tertullian suggests that those troubled in this manner should attend the eucharist, which would take place early in the morning, but rather than receiving Communion at that time they should take the Body of the Lord away, in order to receive Him at the conclusion of the station. The practice of taking the Body of the Lord away for Communion at home was common in third century Africa. Tertullian refers to it at *To His Wife* 2.5, as does Cyprian in *On the Lapsed* 26.

[20]It may be that this military meaning is the origin of the term "station," as used by Tertullian, corresponding to the "vigil" which is kept at night. If this is the case then it is not to be confused with the liturgical stations later kept at Rome. For some discussion of the term see Christine Mohrmann, "Statio," *Vigiliae Christianae*, 7 (1953): 221–245, and Diercks *De Oratione*, 202–5. Mohrmann does not accept that the military meaning is primary, but her suggestion that the term in this sense originates from the Jewish practice of the *ma'amad* is forced, as there is no connection of the *ma'amad* with fasting (Mishnah *Ta'anith* 4:1 makes the distinction clear). Other proferred explanations are criticized by Diercks, namely that the original reference was to the meeting (*statio*) with which the fast ended (criticized on the grounds that the gathering grew out of the fast, rather than vice versa) and that it referred to an accustomed spot at which the fast took place. Diercks prefers the military explanation, but it may be that the military image of a guardpost derived from the custom of keeping the station in a particular place.

[21]The reference is to his work *On the Apparel of Women.*

apostle. Concerning modesty in toilette and adornment there is also the clear direction of Peter who, with the same voice as Paul, because with the same spirit, restrains both vainglorious dress and the pride of gold and the seductive dressing of the hair (1 Pet 3.1–6).

21

But the question of whether virgins should or should not wear the veil is to be discussed as though it were undecided, even though it is a matter of general observation throughout the churches.

Those who allow immunity of the head to virgins seem to make their case on the basis that the apostle does not mention "virgins" but "women" as being veiled, thus not mentioning gender by saying "females" but rather the class of the gender, by saying "women" (1 Cor 11.3–16). For if he had mentioned the gender by saying "females" he would have been laying down a rule for every woman. But since he names only one class of the gender, he is reckoned to say nothing on the other class. For they say that he could have mentioned either virgins specifically or more generally to include them as "females."

22

Those who make this concession need to think again on the meaning of that particular term, on what "woman" means in the first pages of the sacred records. For they shall find that it is the name of a gender, not a class of the gender.

For even when Eve had no knowledge of a man, God had called her both "woman" and "female" (Gen 1.27; 2.23). Thus since Eve, whilst yet unmarried, was described by the term "woman," that term likewise applies to a virgin. So if the apostle, led by that same Spirit by which the book of Genesis, alongside all Scripture, was compiled, has used that same expression, "woman," whilst upholding the unmarried Eve as a pattern which might apply to a virgin, we should not be surprised.

Further considerations fit in with this. By the very fact that he does not name virgins, as he does in another place where he is discussing marriage (1 Cor 7.25), it follows clearly enough that this concerns every woman and that the entire gender is mentioned, and that there is no distinction between a "woman" and a "virgin" (which is not specified at all). For somebody who elsewhere, where the difference demands it, recalls the distinction (for he distinguishes one from another by referring to each class with their proper names) may be understood to have no desire to make the distinction when he does not specify each class by name. Moreover, in the Greek language, which is that employed by the apostle, it is more usual to refer to "women" than to "females," that is to *gunaikes* rather than *thēleiai*. Therefore, if the term that, in translation, stands for that of "female," is in common use as a term to denote gender, he specified the gender when he said *gunē*. A virgin is therefore classified within that gender. Moreover, his meaning, when he says: "Every woman in praying or prophesying with head uncovered is dishonoring her head," is obvious. What is "every woman" if not women of every age and every class and every condition? No woman is excepted when he says "all." In the same way, men are not veiled. For to the same effect he says: "Every man." Therefore, just as the male gender is intended by the term "man," and covering is disallowed even to a young boy, so the female gender is intended by the term "woman," and covering is directed even for a virgin. In both sexes the lesser age should follow the practice of the greater, or else male virgins should be covered if female virgins are not covered, since neither are specifically held under obligation. Otherwise, if the woman were different from the virgin, the boy should be different from the man.

"Does he not say that they should be covered because of the angels, because the angels revolted from God because of human daughters?" (cf. Gen 6.2).

Will anyone now claim that only women, that is to say married women who have left their virginity behind, are objects of desire? Are there no virgins of outstanding beauty who might find lovers?

Rather we might enquire whether they lusted after virgins alone, since Scripture says "human daughters," when it could have specified men's wives, or females without distinction. When it says "They took wives for themselves" it points in that direction, because, of course, those who are taken as wives are free to marry. It might have expressed it otherwise had it concerned those who were not so free. Women are free to marry either by widowhood or by virginity. Therefore by calling the gender, in general terms, "daughters," it includes the species in the genus.

Again: when he says that nature itself teaches that women should be veiled because it has assigned hair to women as a covering and an ornament, is not the same covering and the same decoration of the head ascribed to virgins? If it is shameful for a woman to be shaved, it is no less so for a virgin. Therefore with regard to those to whom a single condition of the head is imputed, a single practice as regards the head is demanded, even among those virgins who are as yet children, for from the first they are denoted with the name of "female." This, moreover, is Israel's practice. But even if it did not so observe, our expanded and completed law might justify adding this law to itself when putting the veil upon virgins. At present, the age that is unaware of its own gender might be excused, having this privilege on account of simplicity. For Eve and Adam alike, when they came to knowledge, immediately covered that of which they had become aware (Gen 3.7), but surely age is under obligation to discipline as to nature among those in whom childhood has moved on, as their bodies and their tasks become those of women. None is a virgin from the time that she can marry, since her age has already married its husband in her, that is time.

"But someone has vowed herself to God!"

However, from that time on she transforms her hair and changes all her clothing to that of a woman. Therefore she should claim to be, and in every respect present herself, as a woman. What she keeps concealed for the sake of God let her keep entirely in the shade. It is to our advantage that we should commend to the knowledge of God what the grace of God has done, rather than that we should receive from people the reward for which we hope from God. Why expose before God what you hide before people? Are you to be more modest in the street than in the church? If indeed it is the grace of God that you have received, "Why," he says, "do you puff yourself up as though you had not received it?" Why do you pass judgment on other women by showing off yourself? Is it that you are inviting other women to the good by your aggrandizement? Rather you are in danger of yourself losing it, if you puff yourself up, whilst driving other women into the same perils. What is built up through self-aggrandizement is readily knocked down. Virgin, veil yourself if virgin you are; to be shamefaced is your duty. If a virgin, shun the glances of many eyes, let nobody gaze upon your face, let nobody be aware of your pretense. It is a good pretense if you cover your head like a married woman, indeed it appears that it is not a pretense, for you are wedded to Christ. To him you have surrendered your body; now act according to your husband's direction. If he commands that the wives of others be covered, so much the more should he command the same of his own.

"But he does not think that the practice instituted by his predecessor should be disturbed."

Many are they who enslave their own prudence and steadfastness to another's custom. Certainly it would not be right to forbid those to take vows who are not in a position to deny that they are virgins standing entirely content and securely on the basis of the knowledge which is with God, whatever rumor might say, just to avoid compulsion in the matter of the veil. But as regards those who are promised to spouses, I may declare firmly, beyond my insignificance, and bear witness that they should be veiled from the day on which first they experience a man through a kiss and through the taking of their right hand.[22] For in these things they are in all respects married already, in age by virtue of maturity, in body by

[22]Tertullian refers here to the rituals of betrothal, the *sponsalia*, which preceded marriage.

virtue of age, in spirit through knowledge, in modesty through experiencing a kiss, in hope through expectation, in mind through the consent they have given. The example of Rebecca is sufficient for us, for her spouse had been no more than pointed out to her when she donned her veil (Gen 24.65), being married simply through knowing who he was.

23

Prayer is also subject to a variety of observance in the matter of bending the knee, for a few will not kneel on the Sabbath.[23] As this debate is even now putting its case to the churches, the Lord will give his grace so that they shall either desist or should have their opinion sustained without giving cause for offense to others.

However, the custom received is that on the Lord's day of resurrection alone we should avoid not only this, but every attitude or activity of concern, postponing business matters as well so that we might yield no place to the Devil. The same is true in the period of the Pentecost, which we likewise mark through the dignity of rejoicing.[24] But on an ordinary day, who would entertain a doubt that he should prostrate himself before God, especially as we enter into daylight with the first of our prayers? On fasting days likewise, and station days, no prayer is to be observed without kneeling and the remaining postures of humility. For then we do not only pray, but beseech and make satisfaction to our Lord God.

24

No rule whatever has been laid down concerning the times of prayer, except, of course, to pray at every time and place (Eph 6.18; 1 Tim

[23]See the first appendix to the introduction for a discussion of this gathering on a Saturday.

[24]Although there was no feast of Pentecost at Tertullian's time, the fifty days after Pascha were observed as days of festivity without fasting.

2.8). But how in every place when we are forbidden prayer in public (Mt 6.5)? In every place, he means, which propriety, or even necessity, suggests. For what the apostles did when they prayed and sang to God in prison as the guards listened (Acts 16.25), or Paul, who made eucharist on a ship in the presence of all (Acts 27.35), is not to be considered contrary to the direction.

25

But concerning time it will not be superfluous to observe those particular hours, I mean those well-known ones which mark the intervals of the day, the third, sixth, and ninth; although from extraneous sources, they are to be found in Scripture as noteworthy.

The Holy Spirit was first poured out on the disciples who were gathered at the third hour (Acts 2.15). Peter had gone onto the rooftop to pray at the sixth hour on the day in which he experienced the vision of everything that is common in that basket (Acts 10.9). And when he went with John to the Temple at the ninth hour he restored the paralyzed man to health (Acts 3.1). Even though, in themselves, these statements have no force in commanding an observance, they are good enough to form the presumption that, bound as we are to pray, they may enforce the obligation and drag us from our business to a period so occupied as though they were a law. As we read that this was Daniel's observance (Dan 6.10), no doubt derived from Israel's practice, thus we may not worship less than three times a day, being debtors of three, the Father and the Son and the Holy Spirit. This, of course, is in addition to the statutory prayers that are due, without particular requirement, at the coming in of the day and of the night.

It is also fitting that the faithful should neither take food nor enter the bath without first interposing a prayer. For the refreshment and sustenance of the spirit should take precedence over those of the flesh, because heavenly things have priority over earthly.

26

Do not let a brother who has entered your house depart without prayer, in particular a stranger, lest he should be, perhaps, an angel (cf. Heb 13.2). For it says: "You have seen a brother—you have seen the Lord."[25] And when you are yourself received by brothers do not give earthly refreshment priority over heavenly; for your faith will be judged at that point. And how should you say, following the direction, "Peace be to this house" (Lk 10.5), unless you give peace to those who are in the house in return for that received.

27

Those who are more conscientious in prayer are accustomed to join "alleluia" and psalms of this sort to their prayers, so that those who are present may respond with their endings.[26] It is an excellent custom to present, like an opulent offering, a prayer fattened with all that tends to dignify and honor God.

28

For this is the spiritual oblation that has wiped out the ancient sacrifices. "What to me is your multitude of sacrifices," he says. "I am filled with holocausts of rams, and I do not want the fat of lambs and the blood of bulls and goats. For who has sought these things from your hands?" (Is 1.11–12). The Gospel teaches the things which God has required. For he says: "The hour will come when true worshippers will worship the Father in spirit and in truth." For "God is spirit" (Jn 4.23–24) and therefore requires worshippers after this nature. We are true worshippers and true priests who, praying in the Spirit, in

[25]The source of this saying is unknown. That a very similar saying is quoted by Clement of Alexandria at *Stromata* 1.19 militates against it being a loose quotation from canonical Scripture. It is possible that it derives from *The Gospel to the Hebrews*.

[26]A practice of responsory psalmody is recorded by Augustine at *Confessions* 9.12.

the spirit offer up prayer, an oblation fitting and acceptable to God, one, indeed, which he has sought, one which he has provided for himself. This we should lead up the altar of God, devoted from the whole heart, fattened with faith, prepared by the truth, spotless in innocence, pure in chastity, garlanded with charity, with a procession of good works as psalms and hymns are sung. This will obtain for us all things from God.

29

For what will God, who so demands, deny to a prayer that derives from the spirit and the truth (Jn 4.24). We read and we hear and we believe in the greatness of the witnesses to its efficacy. Indeed, the old prayer brought deliverance from fire and from wild beasts and from starvation, even though it had not been given shape by Christ. How much more effective, then, is the Christian prayer? It does not situate the angel of dew in the middle of the fire (Dan 3.49–50), nor blocks the mouth of lions (Dan 6.22), nor brings a peasant's dinner to the hungry (Bel 33). By delegated grace it turns away no feeling of pain, but it arms with endurance those who are suffering and knowing pain and grieving. It increases grace with bravery so that faith might know what it obtains from the Lord, understanding what it is suffering for the sake of the name of the Lord. But in times of old prayer summoned plagues (4 Kgs 6.18), put to flight enemy armies (Ex 17.8), withheld the benefits of rain (Jas 5.17). But now the prayer of justice turns away the entire anger of God, keeps watch on behalf of foes, makes supplication for persecutors.[27] Is it a wonder that it knows how to wring water from the heavens,[28] seeing that it would once ignite flames (3 Kgs 18.38)? Prayer alone conquers God. But

---

[27]Cyprian (*On the Lord's Prayer* 17) likewise notes that prayer is made for emperors and persecutors. This would seem to be a reference to the regular intercessions made at the eucharist.

[28]A reference to the tale of the "thundering" legion, Christian soldiers who brought about an end to drought through their prayers, also told by Tertullian at *To Scapula* 4.

Christ has no desire that it should do any evil deed; he has conferred upon it every power of doing good. Therefore it knows only how to call back the souls of the departed from the journey of death itself, to strengthen the weak, to restore the sick, to cleanse the possessed, to open the doors of prison, to loosen the chains of the innocent. The same prayer absolves sins, repels temptations, puts down persecutions, strengthens the weak-hearted, delights the high-minded, leads wanderers home, soothes the waves, confounds robbers, feeds the poor, governs the rich, lifts up the fallen, supports the unsteady, holds firm those who stand. Prayer is the buttress of faith, our armor and weaponry against the enemy that watches us from every side. So never let us set out unarmed—let us remember the station by day and the vigil by night. Let us guard the standard of our emperor armed with prayer, awaiting the trumpet of the angel while we pray. Indeed, every angel prays, every creature. The herds and the wild beasts pray and bend their knees, coming forth from byres and dens looking to heaven, giving movement to the spirit after their fashion with animated mouths. And even now the birds arise, lifting themselves to heaven, spreading out their wings like a cross whilst uttering what appears to be a prayer.[29] What more might be said on the duty of prayer? Even the Lord himself prayed, and to him be honor and might for ever and ever.

[29]E. Evans (*Tertullian's Tract on the Prayer* [London: SPCK, 1953], 61) proposes that the beginning of birdsong is heard even as Tertullian is here declaiming. It is not improbable that the teaching began before dawn (even though this lesson is not delivered at the eucharistic synaxis, as Evans suggests), as this would be a time at which the free poor would be able to attend.

Cyprian: *On the Lord's Prayer*

1

The instructions of the Gospel, dearest brothers, are nothing other than divine commands, foundations on which hope is built, buttresses by which faith is strengthened, food by which the heart is fed, directions by which our journey is guided, bulwarks by which salvation is attained. While they instruct the minds of those who are learning the faith on earth they are leading us to the heavenly Kingdoms. There are many things that God spoke through the prophets, his servants, which he wants us to hear. But how much more would he have us hear those which the Son spoke, to which the Word of God, who was in the prophets, bears witness through his own voice; now not simply ordering that the way of his coming be made ready, but coming himself, showing us and opening to us the way, so that we who previously were wandering, blind, and reckless in the shadow of death, should be illuminated by the light of grace on the journey of life and keep to the way with the Lord as our leader and guide.

2

Among his other saving guidance and divine instructions by which he counselled his people in the way of salvation,[1] he himself gave the form by which to pray, and himself guided and directed the purpose of our prayer. He who brought us to life taught us also to pray, by the kindness out of which he condescended to give and grant other

---

[1] This phrase is echoed by the introduction to the Lord's Prayer in the Roman mass. It is possible, therefore, that the appearance of the phrases here is a liturgical echo, indicating that this part of the Roman mass was African in origin.

things beside. And when we speak with the Father in the prayer and supplication which the Son taught, we may the more readily be heard. He had already said that the hour would come when true worshippers would worship the Father in spirit and in truth (cf. Jn 4.23), and he fulfilled what he had previously promised so that we who receive spirit and truth through his sanctification may truly and spiritually worship through what he has handed on to us.

Indeed, what prayer could be spiritual other than that which Christ, by whom the Holy Spirit is sent to us, has given us? What prayer could be truer in the presence of the Father than that which was conveyed by the Son, who is truth, from his own mouth? That we should pray in a manner distinct from that he taught is not ignorance alone, but is culpable, as he himself affirmed when he said: "You reject the commandment of God, in order to set up your own tradition" (Mk 7.8).

3

Therefore, let us pray, dearest brothers, just as God the master has taught us. Imploring God in his own words, sending up to his ears the prayer of Christ, is a friendly and familiar manner of praying. When we make our prayer let the Father recognize the words of his own Son. May he who lives inside our heart be also in our voice, and since, when as sinners we ask forgiveness of our failings we have him as an advocate for our sins in the presence of the Father (1 Jn 2.1), let us set forth the words of our advocate. For since he said that whatever we ask from the Father in his name he will grant us (Jn 16.23), how much more effectively should we obtain what we ask in the name of Christ if we ask it using his own prayer?[2]

---

[2]The words "Ask and you shall have," apart from the biblical content, were given to Cyprian by Christ in a vision (*Letter* 11.3.1). In this letter Cyprian records that the people did not receive what they sought because they were not united in their petition.

4

However, let the words and the pleas of those who pray be made with discipline, restrained by quiet and reserve. Let us call to mind that we are standing before the face of God. Both the posture of our body and the modulation of our voice should be pleasing to the divine eyes. For whereas the shameless groan and cry out, by contrast it is fitting that the reverent man should pray reserved prayers; for the Lord in his pronouncement commands each of us to pray in secret, in hidden and private places, in our inner rooms (Mt 6.6). This is congruent with our faith, for we know that God is present everywhere, hearing everyone and seeing them, that the plenitude of his majesty penetrates into secluded and hidden places, as it is written: "I am a god who is nearby and not a god who is far off. How might anyone hide in places so secluded that I should not see him? Do I not fill the heaven and the earth?" (Jer 23.23) And again: "The eyes of the Lord look upon the good and the wicked" (Prov 15.3).

And when, together with our brothers, we gather to celebrate the divine sacrifices with the priest of God, we should be mindful of reverence and order,[3] not forever tossing ill-judged phrases into the air, nor seeking to commend our requests by bombarding God with a tumultuous verbosity, because God is a hearer not of the voice but of the heart, nor is he who sees our thoughts prompted by our cries. This the Lord shows us when he says: "Why do you consider evil in your hearts?" (Lk 5.22) And in another place: "Let all the churches know that I am an examiner of the kidney and heart" (Rev 2.23).

---

[3]The term "priest" (*sacerdos*) is reserved to the bishop. Although congregations, particularly in urban areas, might be headed by a priest, Cyprian, in presenting his ideal, is concerned that the catechumens understand that the capstone of the united church is the bishop. Thus this discourse is delivered by the bishop as the normal minister of baptism and post-baptismal hand-laying.

5

Anna, in the first book of Kingdoms, keeps and preserves this rule, so conveying a type of the church.[4] She pleaded with God by crying her petition not out loud but quietly and modestly within her inner heart. She was speaking a secret prayer and made her faith manifest as she spoke, not with her voice but with her heart, since she knew that God would so hear her. He effectually granted what she asked, because she asked in faith. Divine Scripture makes this clear as it says: "She was speaking in her heart and her lips were moving, but her voice was not heard, and God listened to her" (1 Kg 1.13). Again we read in the Psalms: "Speak in your hearts and be remorseful on your beds" (Ps 4.5). The Holy Spirit also suggests the same through Jeremiah and teaches saying: "In the heart, Lord, you are to be worshipped" (Bar 6.6).

6

Moreover the person who prays, dearest brothers, should not be unaware of the manner in which the tax collector prayed in the temple together with the pharisee. He did not brazenly raise his eyes to heaven nor did he insolently raise his hands but, beating his breast and bewailing the sins to be found concealed within, he implored the assistance of the divine mercy. While the pharisee was contented with himself, the one who implored in this manner was the more deserving of sanctification, for he did not place his hope of salvation in relying on his own innocence, for nobody is innocent, but prayed with humility, confessing his sins, and the one who pardons the humble listened to him.

The Lord puts it thus in his Gospel when he states: "Two men went up to the temple to pray, the one a pharisee and the other a tax collector. When the pharisee had taken his place, he prayed by himself in this manner: 'God, I give you thanks because I am not like

[4]Anna also appears as a type of the church in *Testimonies* 1.20.

other men, unjust, grasping, adulterous, as this tax collector is. I fast twice a week, I give tithes on whatever I possess.' The tax collector, however, stood afar off and did not raise his eyes to heaven but beat his breast as he said: 'God be merciful to me a sinner.' I say to you, this man went home justified rather than the pharisee. Because everybody who exalts himself will be humbled, and whoever humbles himself shall be lifted up" (Lk 18.10–14).

7

Dearest brothers, now that we know the manner in which we should approach prayer, having learnt from the divine reading, let us learn the content of our prayer from the Lord our teacher. He says: "Pray thus" (Mt 6.9):

"Our Father, you who are in the heavens, let your name be held holy, let your Kingdom come, let your will be done in heaven and on earth. Give us this day our daily bread and pardon us our debts just as we pardon our debtors; and do not allow us to be led into temptation, but set us free from the evil one."

8

Before all else, the teacher of peace and master of unity desires that we should not make our prayer individually and alone, as whoever prays by himself prays only for himself. We do not say: "My father, who are in the heavens," nor "Give me my bread this day." Nor does anybody request that his debt be pardoned for himself alone, nor ask that he alone be not led into temptation and delivered from the evil one. Our prayer is common and collective, and when we pray we pray not for one but for all people, because we are all one people together. The God of peace and master of concord, who taught that we should be united, wanted one to pray in this manner for all, as he himself bore all in one. The three youths shut up in the furnace of fire observed this law of prayer by joining together in harmony of prayer and agreement of spirit. The reliability of the divine Scriptures declares this; and while it teaches the manner in which they prayed, it gives an example which we should imitate in our prayers, inasmuch as we are able to be like them. It says: "Then those three sang as from one mouth and blessed the Lord" (Dan 3.51). They were speaking as from one mouth and, though Christ had yet to teach them to pray, their speech as they prayed was availing and efficacious because a peaceable and simple and spiritual prayer was pleasing to God.

We find that the apostles, together with the disciples, prayed in this manner after the Lord's ascension. It says: "All were persevering with one mind in their prayer with the women and with Mary who was the mother of Jesus and his brothers" (Acts 1.14). They persevered in prayer, being of one mind in their prayer, as their constancy and unanimity together showed that God, "who causes persons to dwell in a house with one mind" (Ps 67:7), does not admit anyone to the divine and eternal home apart from those whose prayer is of one mind.[5]

9

How great, dearest brothers, are the mysteries of the Lord's Prayer, how many, how magnificent, gathered together in a few words, yet abundant in spiritual power. There is nothing whatever with regard to our pleading and our prayer omitted, nothing not contained in this summary of heavenly doctrine.

"Pray thus," he says: "Our Father, you who are in the heavens." Anybody who is renewed, reborn, and restored to his God by grace, first of all says, "Father," because he is now become a son. It is said: "He came to his own, and his own did not receive him. To as many as did receive him he gave them power to become the children of

---

[5]The same citations and examples of unity recur elsewhere in Cyprian's works, and in particular in *On Unity*. Thus, for the three youths in the furnace, note *On Unity* 12; for the unity of the apostles in prayer, note *On Unity* 25; for the citation of Ps 67.7, *On Unity* 8.

God, who believe in his name" (Jn 1.11). Whoever therefore believes in his name is made a child of God, and hence should begin to give thanks and show himself a child of God as he names his Father as God in heaven. He bears witness also, among the first of his words at his rebirth,[6] that he renounces his earthly and fleshly father and acknowledges that he has begun to have the Father in heaven as his only father, as it is written: "Those who say to father and mother 'I do not know you,' and recognize not their own children, these will keep your commands and observe your covenant" (Deut 33.9). Again the Lord, in his Gospel, commands that we should call nobody "father" on earth, because we have one Father who is in heaven. And to his disciple who made mention of his departed father he replied: "Let the dead bury their dead" (Mt 8.22). For he had said that his father was dead, while the Father of believers is alive.

10

Dearest brothers, we should turn our minds and understand not only that we call him "Father who is in heaven," but that we add to this and say: "Our Father," that is of those who believe, of those who have begun to be children of God, sanctified through him and restored by a birth of spiritual grace. This word also upbraids and accuses the Jews, because Christ was proclaimed to them through the prophets and was sent first to them. They not only despised him in their unbelief, but also cruelly did him to death. So no longer now can they call the Lord their father, for the Lord confounds and refutes them saying: "You are born of your father, the devil, and desire to do the pleasure of your father. For he was a murderer from the beginning and stood not in truth, because truth is not in him" (Jn 8.44). And God cries out with anger through Isaiah the prophet:

---

[6]An allusion to the practice of praying the Lord's Prayer immediately after baptism is turned to become a retrospective witness to the renunciation that had already taken place, as the family networks of which the candidate was previously part have been renounced in order to enter the household of the church.

"I have begotten sons and brought them up, but they have despised me. An ox recognizes his owner and an ass the crib of his master. But Israel has not known me and the people have not understood me. Alas! A race of sin, a people full of sin, a worthless seed, abominable children. You have abandoned the Lord and provoked the Holy One of Israel to anger" (Is 1.3–4).

We Christians hold them guilty when we say: "Our Father," because he has now begun to be ours and ceased to be the Father of the Jews, who abandoned him. Nor can a sinful people be a child, but the name of children is ascribed to those to whom the remission of sins is given, and to them is eternity promised by God himself as he says: "Whoever sins is a slave. A slave, however, does not remain forever in the house, but the son remains forever" (Jn 8.34).

11

So great is the mercy of the Lord, so abundant his condescension and goodness, that he desired that we should make our prayer in this manner in the sight of God, that we should address the Lord as "Father," and that we should be considered sons of God, as Christ is the son of God. None of us would have dared use this name in prayer except that he has authorized us to pray after this manner. We should remember, therefore, dearest brothers, and realize that when we address God as our Father we should act as children of God, so that just as we have pleasure in having God as our Father, so he should have pleasure in us. Let us act as temples of God,[7] so that it may appear that God dwells in us. Let our conduct not fall away from the spirit; rather, we, who have begun to be spiritual and heavenly, should think and perform spiritual and heavenly things. As the Lord God himself has said: "I shall honor those who honor me; and those who disregard me shall I disregard" (1 Kg 2.30). The blessed apostle,

---

[7]This allusion to 1 Cor 6.19 recalls a similar allusion at *Letter* 13.5, which deals with the subject of confessors sharing a bed with virgins. This practice is discussed and condemned by Cyprian in *Letter* 4.

in his letter, states: "You are not your own, for you were bought at a great price. Honor and carry God in your body" (1 Cor 6.20).

12

Next we say: "Let your name be hallowed." We say this not wishing that God should be made holy by our prayers, but asking the Lord that his name should be hallowed in us. Indeed, how could God, who is himself the one who hallows, be hallowed? As he said himself: "Be holy, as I too am holy" (Lev 20.7). We ask and beseech that we who are made holy in baptism should have the ability to persist in the way we have begun. And we request this every day. Our need is of daily sanctification, so that we who daily fail should have our sins purged by continual hallowing.[8] The apostle states the nature of the hallowing which is conveyed to us from the grace of God when he says: "Neither fornicators, nor idolaters, nor adulterers, nor the effeminate, nor sodomizers, nor thieves, nor cheats, nor drunkards, nor wizards, nor the rapacious, shall attain to the Kingdom of God. Indeed, you were all of these, but you have been washed, you have been made just, you have been hallowed in the name of the Lord Jesus Christ and in the Spirit of our God" (1 Cor 6.9). He says that we have been hallowed in the name of the Lord Jesus Christ and in the Spirit of our God and we in turn, because our master and judge warns the one who has been healed and revived by him to sin no more lest something worse should befall him (Jn 5.14), pray that this hallowing should remain within us. We make this plea in continuous prayer; we ask day and night that the hallowing and revival which has been received from the grace of God should be preserved by his protecting care.

---

[8]The same point is made to catechumens by Augustine *Sermon to Catechumens* 15: "We are cleansed once in baptism, we are cleansed daily by the prayer."

13

There follows in the Prayer: "Let your Kingdom come." Just as we desire that his name be hallowed among us, we ask that the Kingdom of God be made known to us. For when does God not reign, or when does that which always was, and shall never cease to be, begin? We ask that our Kingdom, promised us by God, may come, won by Christ's blood and passion, so that we who have served him in the world should afterward come to reign with Christ as Lord, as he himself promises and says: "Come, blessed of my Father, receive the Kingdom prepared for you from the foundation of the world" (Mt 25.34).

It is indeed possible, beloved brothers, that Christ himself is that Kingdom whose coming we daily desire, whose coming we desire soon to see. For since he is himself the resurrection, because we shall rise in him, so we may understand that he is himself the Kingdom of God, because in him we are to reign. Also we do well to ask for the Kingdom of God, that is the heavenly Kingdom, because there is an earthly kingdom, but whoever now renounces the world is greater than its honors and its kingdom alike. And therefore whoever commends himself to God and Christ is seeking not after earthly kingdoms but heavenly. And our labor of prayer and petition is ceaseless, lest we should be excluded from the heavenly realm as the Jews, to whom it had first been promised, were excluded, as the Lord made clear and showed. For "Many," he says, "shall come from the east and the west and shall sit down with Abraham and Isaac and Jacob in the Kingdom of heaven. However, the sons of the Kingdom shall be cast into outer darkness, where there will be wailing and gnashing of teeth" (Mt 8.11). He points out that previously the Jews were the sons of the Kingdom, as long as they continued to be children of God. But when the name of the Father was abandoned among them, the Kingdom was abandoned as well. And thus we Christians, who in prayer have begun to call on God as the Father, pray that the Kingdom of God might likewise come to us.

14

We go on to say: "Let your will be done in heaven and on earth." We say this not so that God might do what he wishes, but that we should be able to do what God wishes. For who stands in the way of God to prevent him performing his will? But since we are opposed by the Devil, and our thought and deeds are so prevented from complete submission to God, we pray requesting that the will of God might be done in us. For this to be done in us there is need of God's will, that is his aid and his protection, since nobody is strong in his own strength, but is kept safe in God's kindness and mercy. And so, even the Lord, showing the human weakness which he bore, says: "Father, if it might be possible, let this cup pass away from me" (Mt 26.39). And, providing an example to his disciples that they should do not their own will but that of God, he went on to say: "Nonetheless not what I desire but that which you desire." And he says in another place: "I have not come down from heaven to do my own will but the will of him who sent me" (Jn 6.38). Now if the Son was obedient in the performance of his Father's will, how much more should the servant be obedient in doing the will of his master. So John exhorts to the performance of the will of God and gives instruction saying: "Do not love the world, nor the things which are in the world. If anybody loves the world, the love of the Father is not in him, because everything in the world is lust of the flesh and lust of the eyes and pride in this present age, which are not from the Father but are come from worldly desire. And the world and its desires will pass away. Yet whoever does the will of God shall remain into eternity just as God remains into eternity" (1 Jn 2.15). We who desire to remain into eternity should do the will of God who is eternal.

15

Now the will of God is that which Christ both did and taught. Humility in conduct, constancy in faith, truth in speech, justice in deeds, mercy in works, restraint in self-discipline, knowing nothing of doing injury yet willing to endure slight, holding to peace with the brothers, devoted wholeheartedly to the Lord, loving him as Father, fearing him as God, preferring nothing whatsoever to Christ because he preferred nothing to ourselves, clinging inseparably to his love, standing by his cross with courage and faith, and, when his name and honor are contested, being a confessor by constancy in what we say, being defiant by fidelity under interrogation, receiving the crown by patience under sentence of death. This is the desire to be co-heir with Christ, this is the performance of the command of God, this is the fulfillment of the Father's will.

16

We ask that the will of God be done in heaven and on earth. Each pertains to the completion of our safety and salvation. For since we are in possession of a body from the earth and a spirit from heaven we are ourselves both earth and heaven, and we pray therefore that the will of God be done in both, that is both in our body and in our spirit. For there is strife between the flesh and the spirit, a daily contest as they clash with one another so that we do not the things we desire. While the spirit seeks the things that are heavenly and godly, the flesh lusts after the things which are earthly and worldly; and therefore we ask that reconciliation be brought about between the two through the help and assistance of God, and so, while the will of God is undertaken both in the spirit and in the flesh, the soul which is reborn through him may be saved. This Paul the apostle in his own words declares openly and plainly, as he says, "The flesh hankers after those things which oppose the spirit and the spirit hankers against the flesh. These things are opposed to one another so that you do not do the very things that you desire. The works of the flesh are obvious, for they are adultery, fornication, impurity, filthiness, idolatry, poisoning, murder, enmity, strife, rivalry, antipathy, provocation, jealousy, dissension, sectarianism, envy, drunkenness, revelry and suchlike things. Such things as this will not possess the Kingdom of God. However, the fruit of the spirit is love, rejoicing, peace, magnanimity, goodness, faith, gentleness, continence, chastity" (Gal 5.17). And so we pray daily, or rather unceasingly, the prayer that the will of God be done around us both in heaven and on earth. Because it is the will of God that earthly things should yield to heavenly, that the spiritual and godly should prevail.

17

It may also be understood, dearest brothers, that just as the Lord commands and counsels us to love even our enemies and also to pray for those who persecute us (Mt 5.44), so we pray also for those who are still earth, and have not yet embarked upon being heavenly, and pray that the will of God be done among them, as did Christ in his salvation and restoration of humanity. For since the disciples are no longer called "earth" by him but "salt of the earth" (Mt 5.13), and the apostle states that the first man is from the dust of the earth, but that the second is from the heaven (1 Cor 15.47), it is fitting that we should be like God the Father, who causes the sun to rise on the good and the wicked, and rains on the just and the unjust (Mt 5.45); and so we should pray and intercede as Christ counsels us, and make intercession for the salvation of all,[9] so that just as the will of God is done in heaven, that is in us, through our faith, with the result that we are in heaven, so also the will of God should be done on earth, that is among those who do not believe, so that those who are earthly from their original birth should begin to be heavenly, being born of water and the Spirit (Jn 3.5).

[9]As noted at Tertullian *On Prayer* 29, the intercessions of the eucharist included intercession for the emperor. Further witness is borne to this by Tertullian at *Apology* 30 and Cyprian himself in the *Proconsular Acts* 1.

18

As the Prayer proceeds we ask and say: "Give us this day our daily bread." This may be understood both spiritually and literally, since both understandings may lead to salvation through the divine plan. For Christ is the bread of life (Jn 6.48), and thus he is not the bread of anybody but ourselves. And in the same way that we say "Our Father," since he is the Father of those who have knowledge and belief, so we refer to "our" bread, since Christ is the bread of those who participate in his body.

Moreover we ask that this bread should be given to us daily lest we who are in Christ, and receive his eucharist daily as the food of salvation,[10] should be prevented by the interposition of some terrible sin and so be separated from the Body of Christ, inhibited from and not receiving the heavenly bread.[11] This he himself taught when he said: "I am the bread of life which came down from heaven. If anyone should eat of my bread he shall live forever. And the bread which I shall give is my flesh for the life of the world" (Jn 6.51). Thus, when he says that anyone who eats of his bread will live forever, so making it clear that those who participate in his body and receive the eucharist, communicating by right, are those who live. So we are to pray in fear, lest anyone should be inhibited and so separated from the body of Christ, thus being put far from salvation. He warns us himself when he says: "Unless you eat the flesh of the son of man and drink his blood you shall not have life in you" (Jn 6.53). Consequently, we ask that we be given our bread, that is Christ, daily, so

[10]This may indicate a daily celebration of the eucharist (to which witness is borne in *Letter* 53.3), but may equally refer to a daily reception of the eucharist at home, as described by Tertullian at *To His Wife* 2.5, and to which there is oblique reference at Tertullian *On Prayer* 6.

[11]Because the eucharist was a representation of the heavenly banquet, as the church was a model of heavenly society, those doing penance were excluded from Communion. A terrible sin, particularly murder, but also idolatry, until the case of the lapsed was reconsidered, led to exclusion for life, with the hope of reconciliation at the time of death.

that we may remain in Christ, and live through his sanctification, and fall not away from his body.

19

It is also possible to understand the request thus: that we who have renounced the world and its wealth and its pomp,[12] abandoning them through faith in his spiritual grace, are asking for as much food and sustenance as is needful. As the Lord instructed us and said: "Whoever does not renounce all that is his cannot be my disciple" (Lk 14.33).

Anyone who has begun to be a disciple of Christ, renouncing all things according to the demand of his master, needs to ask for his daily food, and not to extend the desires for which he prays into the future. Again the Lord instructs us and says: "Do not give consideration to the morrow, for the morrow will give consideration to itself. The wickedness of a day is sufficient for itself" (Mt 6.34). Very properly, therefore, does the disciple of Christ, who is forbidden to give consideration for the morrow, ask for sustenance for himself for that one day. It would be a contradictory and negative thing were we, who ask that the Kingdom of God come quickly, to seek to live a long time in this present age. So the blessed apostle counsels, as he builds and buttresses the foundation of our hope and faith. "We brought nothing," he says, "into this world and we certainly can take nothing out. Therefore having food and clothing we are content with these. Those who wish to become rich fall into temptation and snares and many harmful desires that drown a person in perdition and in ruin. For the root of all evils is cupidity; some, seeking it, have been shipwrecked from the faith and made many sorrows for themselves" (1 Tim 6.7).

---

[12]An allusion to the words of renunciation, said before the candidate for baptism enters the waters.

20

He teaches not only that wealth is to be despised but that it is dangerous, and hence that it is the root of seductive evils, which by their covert falsity deceive the blindness of the human mind. Hence God declared guilty the rich fool as he was regarding his worldly hoard and rejoicing in the richness of his abundant harvests. "You fool, your soul will be demanded of you tonight. Whose then will be the things you have provided?" (Lk 12.20) The fool, rejoicing in his harvests, was to die that night and was thinking of his plentiful provisions even as his life was running out. By contrast, the Lord teaches us that the one who is perfect and complete sells all he has and gives it up for the poor,[13] so providing himself with a treasury in heaven (Mt 19.21). He says that the one who is unencumbered and tightly girt and not ensnared by the traps of property is able to follow him and imitate the glory of the Lord's passion. Released and set free he accompanies his own possessions that he had previously sent on to the Lord. So that each of us is able to prepare himself, he teaches us to pray in this manner and to know through the terms of the prayer what sort of person he should be.

21

The just man will not go without daily food, as it is written: "The Lord will not allow the just man to starve" (Prov 10.3), and again: "I have been young and now I am old, and I have not seen the just man destitute nor his seed begging for bread" (Ps 36.25). The Lord makes a promise as he says: "Do not worry, saying 'What shall we eat or what shall we drink or what shall we wear?' For the gentiles seek these things. However, your Father knows that you are in need of all these things. Seek first the Kingdom and the righteousness of God,

---

[13]Pontius informs us that Cyprian, as a catechumen, divested himself of vast wealth (*Life* 2), though Cyprian continues to hold some personal wealth that is used for the good of the church.

and all these things shall be provided for you" (Mt 6.31). He promises to provide everything for those who seek the Kingdom and the righteousness of God for, since all things are God's, the one who has God will lack nothing if he is not lacking in God. So too Daniel, locked in the lions' den at the king's command, was providentially provided with a meal,[14] and the man of God was fed among hungry, yet abstinent, wild beasts! Elijah in his solitary flight was fed by ministering ravens and was nourished amidst persecution by birds who brought him food (3 Kg 17.6). The lions were merciful, the birds brought food,—and men lay snares and savagely attack. How detestable the cruelty of human evil!

22

After this we implore on account of our sins as we say: "And pardon us our debts, just as we pardon our debtors." After asking for the supply of food we ask pardon for our sin, so that the one who is fed by God may live in God, and provision be made not only for this present and transitory life but for the eternal life to which we might come if our sins are pardoned. These the Lord calls debts, as it says in his Gospel: "I have forgiven you every debt because you requested me" (Mt 18.32). How necessarily, how properly and prudently, are we reminded that we are sinners and are under obligation to ask on account of our sins so that, whilst the mercy of God is being sought, the mind may be recalled to a sense of its guilt. Lest anyone be self-satisfied, thinking himself innocent, and should perish once again because of his boasting, he is informed and instructed daily that he is a sinner, being commanded to make prayer daily on account of his sins. So John counsels in his letter: "If we say that we have no sin we are deceiving ourselves and the truth is not in us. If, however, we make confession of our sins, the Lord is faithful and just and forgives our sins" (1 Jn 1.8). In his letter both parts are included, that is that

---

[14]Dan 6.16–17. No mention is made of a meal in this text.

we should implore on account of our sins and that we should obtain pardon in asking. Therefore he says that God is faithful in forgiving sins, for he faithfully keeps the promise that he has made that the Father's mercy and pardon would come to us who make our prayers on account of our debts and sins.

23

The Savior added and affixed a clear rule, binding us by an assured condition and pledge, that just as we ask that our debts should be pardoned, following this we ourselves pardon those who are in debt to us.

We know that we cannot obtain that for which we ask on account of our sins unless we ourselves do the same for those who have sinned against us. Therefore he also says in another place: "With whatever measure you have measured, in that shall it be measured out for you" (Mt 7.2). And the servant, after his entire debt was remitted by his master, was thrown into prison when he refused to pardon his fellow servant (Mt 18.34). Because he refused pity to his fellow servant he lost that pity which had been offered him by his master. Christ sets this forth in his instruction yet more firmly and rebukes us the more forcefully when he says: "When you are standing at prayer, pardon whatever you may have against anybody, so that your Father who is in heaven may forgive your sins. If, however, you will not pardon, neither will your Father who is in heaven pardon you your sins" (Mk 11.25). On the day of judgment no excuse will remain to you, should you be judged in accordance with the sentence you have passed, and you will suffer whatever you have meted out. The Lord instructs you, therefore, to be peaceable and agreeable and of one mind in his house.[15] He wishes that we should remain as we are when we are reborn in our second birth, that those who are children of God should remain in the peace of God, and that those

---

[15]Ps. 67:7; cf. ch. 8 above.

who are in possession of one spirit should possess one mind and heart. Thus God does not accept the sacrifice of one who is in dispute, and sends him back from the altar, ordering him first to be reconciled to his brother, so that he may pacify God by praying as a peacemaker. The greater sacrifice to God is our peace and brotherly agreement, as a people unified in the unity of the Father and the Son and the Holy Spirit.[16]

24

For when Abel and Cain first offered sacrifices, God did not look upon their gifts but upon their hearts, and the one who pleased him was pleasing in his heart (cf. Gen 4.3–5). Abel was peaceable and just, and as he sacrificed in innocence so he taught others that, when they offer their gifts at the altar, they should come with fear of God, with simplicity of heart, with accustomed justice, with peace and reconciliation. And he whose character was such when he sacrificed received the reward of being himself a sacrifice to God. The one who held to the Lord's justice and peace was the first to show us martyrdom, and to inaugurate the Lord's passion through the glory of his blood.

Persons of this character are crowned by the Lord, and in the day of judgment will be judges with the Lord,[17] whereas the one who is disruptive and disagreeable and is not at peace with the brothers, even though he be put to death for the name, shall not be able to escape the charge of hostility toward the brothers. This is in accordance with the witness of the blessed apostle and of holy Scripture, for, as it is written: "Whoever hates his brother is a murderer"

[16]Réveillaud, *Saint Cyprien*, 192–193, finds a liturgical echo here, as Cyprian (*Letter* 63.13) describes the admixture of water and wine in the chalice as the admixture of the people with Christ.

[17]An alternative reading is "Will be avenged." Whereas this reading is close to Rev 6.10, the text translated here fits the context better. A similar point about the martyr being judge with Christ in the heavenly tribunal is found elsewhere in Cyprian's correspondence (e.g. *Letter* 6.2.1; 31.3 [to Cyprian]).

(1 Jn 3.15). A murderer shall not attain to the Kingdom of heaven, nor shall he live with God. Whoever prefers to follow Judas, rather than Christ, cannot be with Christ. What an offense, which cannot be wiped out by the baptism of blood! What a crime, which cannot be expunged by martyrdom![18]

25

Beyond this, the Lord, of necessity, counsels that we should say: "Do not allow us to be led into temptation" in our prayer.[19] We are shown in this clause that the adversary can do nothing against us unless God allows it beforehand. Thus all our fear and our devotion and our heedfulness should be directed toward God, so that he when we are in temptation he allow no power to the evil one apart from that which he grants.

So Scripture demonstrates when it says: "Nebuchadnezzar the King of Babylon came up against Jerusalem and attacked it and the Lord delivered it into his hand" (4 Kg 24.11). For power against us is given to the evil one in proportion to our sins, as it is written: "Who gave Jacob over to pillage and Israel to those who plundered him? Was it not God, against whom they sinned, refusing to walk in his ways or to hear his law? And he has poured out the rage of his provocation upon them" (Is 42.25). And again, when Solomon sinned and fell away from the instructions and the ways of the Lord, it is recorded: "And the Lord stirred up Satan against Solomon" (3 Kg 11.14).

---

[18] It is indicative of how serious Cyprian considers to be the crime of schism that here he is prepared to contradict Tertullian, who states that martyrdom can wipe out any sin (*Apology* 50.16; *Scorpiace* 6; *On the Soul* 55).

[19] Although Tertullian cites this petition in a different form (see *On Prayer* 8 and the third appendix to the introduction) he gives this form as a paraphrase. Significantly, this form seems close to that employed in the Marcionite Gospel, cited by Tertullian at *Against Marcion* 4.26.5.

26

For two reasons is power granted against us: for punishment when we sin and for glory when we are proved. This is what we see in the case of Job, for God makes this clear when he says: "Look, everything that he has I give into your hands. But be sure that you do not touch the man himself" (Job 1.12). And the Lord, on the occasion of his suffering, says in the Gospel: "You would have no power against me unless it were given you from above" (Jn 19.11).

So when we ask that we should not come into temptation we are reminded of our frailty and weakness even as we are making the request, lest anyone should insolently puff himself up, lest anyone should proudly and arrogantly take anything to himself, lest anyone should arrogate to himself the glory of being a confessor or of suffering, for the Lord himself taught humility when he said: "Watch and pray, lest you come to temptation. For the spirit is ready but the flesh is weak" (Mt 26.41). Thus precedence is given to a humble and submissive confession, and everything is referred to God so that whatever is sought out of the fear of God and is requested with a view to his honor will be granted out of his goodness.

27

After all of this there comes a phrase, in conclusion of the Prayer, which gathers the sum of our prayers and requests into a short summary. For at the very end we say: "But set us free from the evil one." This includes all the weapons that the enemy brings up against us in this world, from which we are sure to find security and safety if God set us free. If we pray and beseech he will show us his succor.

However, when we have said: "Set us free from the evil one" there remains nothing which should be sought thereafter. For when we have requested the protection of God against the evil one, and when it is granted, we stand secure and safe against everything that the devil and the world may do against us. Who can be afraid of the present world when God in the present world is his protector?

28

Dearest brothers, why wonder that the prayer which the Lord taught should be of such a nature, that through his instruction in a saving phrase he sums up our entire prayer? This had already been foretold in advance through the prophet Isaiah when he, full of the Holy Spirit, spoke of the majesty and the goodness of God. He said: "Summing up the word and cutting it short in his justice, so that God may make a short word in all the earth" (Is 10.22). For when the Word of God, our Savior Jesus Christ, came and gathered the learned along with the unlearned and handed over the commands of salvation to every sex and age, he made a sublime summary of his commands so that the memory of his disciples should not be taxed by the holy rule but that they should speedily learn what is necessary for a simple faith. So, when he taught concerning eternal life, the mystery of life was contained in a deep and divine brevity when he said: "This is eternal life, that they should know you, the only true God, and Jesus Christ whom you have sent" (Jn 17.3). Again when he gathered from the law and the prophets the first and greatest commandment he said: " 'Hear Israel: The Lord your God is one, and you shall love the Lord your God with all your heart and with all your mind and with all your strength.' This is the first commandment. And the second is similar to this: 'you shall love your neighbor as yourself'; on these two commands hang the entire law and the prophets" (cf. Mk 12.29–31 and Mt 22.37–40). And again: "Whatever of good you wish that others should do to you, so do you to them. For this is the law and the prophets" (Mt 7.12).

29

Not by words alone but by deeds does God teach us to pray. He himself prayed frequently, pleading and showing us what we ought to do by the testimony of his example, as it is written: "He took himself away to a deserted place to pray" (Lk 5.16) and again: "He went up the mountain to pray and spent the night in prayer to God" (Lk 6.12). If he who was without sin would pray, how much the more should sinners pray, and if he kept continual vigil and prayed with unceasing prayer throughout the night, how much the more should we spend the night keeping watch with constant prayer.[20]

3 0

Now the Lord was praying and pleading not for himself, what indeed would he want for, innocent as he was, but for our sins, just as he himself made plain when he said to Peter: "Look, Satan was asking that he should sift you like wheat. I, however, have asked on your behalf that your faith should not fail you" (Lk 22.31). And afterward he pleaded with the Father for all people when he said: "I do not pray for these alone but for those who shall believe in me through their word, that they should all be one; just as you, Father are in me and I in you, so should they be in us" (Jn 17.20). So great are the kindness and the fidelity alike of God, with regard to our salvation, that he was not content simply to redeem us through his own blood but beyond this that he should plead for us so fully. You may see what was the desire of him who pleaded, that just as the Father and the Son are one, so we likewise should remain in the selfsame unity. And thus it may also be understood how great a sin it is to tear apart unity and peace, because the Lord prayed for this very thing, desiring that his people should have life, knowing that discord does not enter the Kingdom of God.

31

Now when we stand to pray,[21] dearest brothers, we should be watch-ful and apply ourselves to our prayers with our whole heart. Every

---

[20]A reference, perhaps, to the vigil which is about to be undertaken. See the invi-tation to keep vigil at the conclusion of this address, and the final endnote.

[21]Although the audience would be standing in any event before the eucharist, the standing might be a standing to attention.

fleshly and worldly thought should depart, nor should any mind dwell on anything other than the prayer that it is offering. Therefore, before the prayer, the priest prepares the minds of the brothers by first uttering a preface as he says: "Hearts on high!" And as the people reply: "We have them to the Lord,"[22] so they are warned that they should think of nothing other than the Lord. The heart is closed against the enemy and lies open to God alone, so that the foe of God might not enter at a time of prayer. For he creeps around constantly and insinuates himself with subtlety, deceitfully calling away our prayers from God, so that we have one thing in our heart and another on our lips. It is not the sound of our voice but the mind and the heart which should pray to God with sincere intent. What lethargy it is to be led astray and captured by unbecoming and profane thoughts when you are praying to the Lord, as though there were some matter to which you should give more attention than what you are saying to God! How can you expect God to hear you when you yourself cannot hear? Do you want God to have you in mind when you are making prayer when you are not even mindful of yourself? This is to be entirely off-guard before the enemy, this, when you pray to God, is to cause offense to the majesty of God through your neglectful prayer, this is to be watchful with your eyes yet drowsy in your heart when a Christian should be watchful in his heart whilst sleeping with his eyes. As it is written in the Song of Songs in the character of the church: "I am asleep and my heart is awake" (Song 5.2). The apostle counsels us with solicitude and anxiety when he says: "Continue in prayer and be watchful at it" (Col 4.2). That is, he is teaching those who are watchful in their prayer and showing them what can be gained by those who ask of God.

---

[22]Although this same greeting appears at the eucharist, followed by a call to give thanks, the absence of a call to thanksgiving may imply that what is reported here is not the opening of the eucharistic prayer. On the other hand, according to *Apostolic Tradition* 25, "hearts on high" is said only at the offering, and the fact that the bishop (the word "priest" without qualification is employed by Cyprian only of the bishop) is the celebrant indicates that the eucharist is meant.

32

Those who pray should not come to God with unfruitful or barren prayers. A request is futile when a sterile prayer is made to God. For just as every tree that does not bear fruit is cut down and thrown into the fire (Mt 7.19), so an utterance that has no fruit cannot be well-pleasing to God because it does not supply any works. And so the divine Scripture instructs us when it says: "A prayer with fasting and almsgiving is good" (Tobit 12.8). For he who, in the day of judgment, shall return a reward for works and almsgiving is a kindly listener today to the prayer of one who comes to him in prayer associated with good deeds. Thus, for instance, Cornelius the centurion deserved to be heard when he prayed. For he was a frequent giver of alms to the people and prayed constantly to God. Thus around the ninth hour, when he was at prayer, an angel was standing by, bearing witness to his good deeds and saying: "Cornelius, your prayers and almsgiving have ascended as a memorial before God" (Acts 10.2–4).

33

The prayers that ascend quickly to God are those which the merits of our works urge upon him. So said the angel Raphael as he stood before Tobias, who was constant in prayer and good deeds: "It is honorable to make known and to confess the works of God. For when you and Sara prayed I bore the recollection of your prayer into the presence of the holiness of God. And when you buried the dead as a simple duty, and because you did not hold back from getting up and leaving your meal, but departed to cover the dead, I was sent to try you. And again God sent me to heal you and Sara your daughter-in-law. For I am Raphael, one of the seven righteous angels who stand and minister before the holiness of God" (Tobit 12.11).

The Lord also counsels and teaches us through Isaiah, bearing witness to similar matters: "Release," he says "every knot of unrighteousness, and undo the oppression of invalid contracts. Send away the feeble in peace and annul every unjust agreement. Break your bread for the hungry and bring into your home the homeless poor. If you see anyone naked, clothe him, and do not despise the household of your own seed. Then shall your light break forth in season, and your clothing shall quickly arise and your justice shall go before you and the holiness of God shall surround you. Then you shall cry out, and God will give ear to you. Then, as soon as you speak, he shall say: 'Look, I am here' " (Is 58.6). He promises that he will be present and says that he hears and protects those who loosen the knots of unrighteousness from their hearts, and who give alms to the servants of God, and act in accordance with his directions. Those who hear what God demands should be done will themselves merit a hearing from God.

The blessed apostle Paul, when assisted by the brothers in the stress of persecution, said that the works that they performed were sacrifices to God. He says: "I am filled, having received those things which were sent by you from Epaphroditus, a sweet odor, a sacrifice acceptable and pleasing to God" (Phil 4.18). For anyone who has pity on a poor man has lent to God (Prov 19.17), and whoever gives to the little ones gives to God, spiritually sacrificing sweet odors to God.

34

In celebrating our prayers we may observe that the three children, together with Daniel, who were strong in faith and victorious in their captivity, observed in their prayer the third, the sixth, and the ninth hour (cf. Dan 6.10) as a figure, as it were, of the Trinity which should be made manifest in more recent times. For the progress of the first hour to the third shows the completed number of the trinity, and the sixth hour, progressing from the fourth, declares another Trinity, and when the seventh to the ninth is completed the perfect trinity is accounted through three-hour periods. Long ago, spiritual worshippers of God fixed upon these periods of time and observed them as times appointed and lawful for prayer.[23]

[23]The actual times are not specified in Daniel; Cyprian simply assumes that the

Subsequent events have shown that these were mysteries, in that the just formerly prayed in this way. For the Spirit came down upon the disciples at the third hour, filling them with the grace promised by the Lord (Acts 2.15). Likewise Peter, going up onto the roof at the sixth hour was instructed by a sign and by the voice of God, directing that he should admit all to the grace of salvation (Acts 10.9), since he had formerly doubted whether gentiles should be cleansed. And at the sixth hour the Lord was crucified and at the ninth he washed away our sins by his blood (Mk 15.33–34) and, so that he could redeem us and give us life, he then perfected the victory by his passion.

35

Dearest brothers, for us both the times and the dispensations have increased beyond those observed for prayer of old. For we should pray in the morning in order that the resurrection of the Lord should be celebrated in morning prayer. This the Holy Spirit previously pointed out in the Psalms, when he said: "My king and my God! I will pray to you, O Lord, in the morning and you will hear my voice. In the morning I shall stand before you and I shall see you" (Ps 5.4). And again the Lord speaks through the prophet: "Early in the morning they will watch for me and say: 'Let us go and return to the Lord our God'" (Hos. 6:1). When the sun goes down and at the close of the day it is necessary for us to pray again. For, because Christ is the true sun and the true day, when we pray at the decline of the sun and the day of this present world, and ask that light may again come upon us, we are praying that the coming of Christ should reveal to us the grace of eternal light.[24] The Holy Spirit declares in the Psalms that Christ is called "the day" when he says: "The stone which the builders rejected is become the head of the

three hours are those familiar to him. See the second appendix to the introduction for further discussion and references.

[24]As noted at Tertullian *On Prayer* 5, it is possible, given the common wording of the two, that this is a citation of an actual prayer in use at Carthage.

corner. This has been done by the Lord and is marvelous in our eyes. This is the day which the Lord made; let us rejoice and feast in it" (Ps 117.22–24). Again, that he is called "The sun" is witnessed by Malachi the prophet as he says: "The sun of justice shall arise upon you who fear the name of the Lord, and healing is in his wings" (Mal 4.2). But if, in the holy Scriptures, Christ is the true sun and the true day, God should be worshipped constantly and continually. There is no hour at which Christians should not pray; rather, since we are in Christ, that is, in the true sun and the true day, we should spend the entire day in petition and prayer. And when, by the law of the world in its recurrent changes, night's turn comes on, then, since to the children of light night itself is as day, we are not to cease from prayer in the darkness of the night. For when are we, who have the light in our hearts, without light? Or when is the one to whom Christ is the sun and the day without the sun and without the day?

36

Those of us who are in Christ, that is in the light, should not cease from prayer even at night. Thus Anna, a widow, persevered without interruption, constant in prayer and pleasing God in keeping vigil. Thus it is written in the Gospel: "She did not depart from the temple, serving night and day with fasting and prayer" (Lk 2.37). That there remain pagans who are still unenlightened or Jews who have left the light for the darkness is no concern to us. We, dearest brothers, who are constantly in the light of the Lord, we who recall and hold fast to what we have begun to receive by grace, should reckon night as daytime; we believe that we are constantly walking in the light, so let us not be hindered by the darkness from which we have escaped. There should be no lack of prayer in the hours of the night, no idle and shiftless waste of occasions for prayer. Through the mercy of God we have been spiritually remade and so, when we are reborn, let us imitate what we are destined to become. For since, in the Kingdom, we shall have the day alone, without the interruption of the night, let us keep nocturnal vigil as though in the light.[25] And since we shall pray constantly and give thanks to God, let us not cease here likewise to pray and to give thanks.

[25]As opposed to the reference to birdsong at the conclusion of Tertullian's treatise, which having been edited through the expansion of an address at the *traditio orationis* implies a setting of more general teaching, the reference to a forthcoming vigil implies that this was the context of the *traditio orationis*, namely that after the *redditio symboli* on a Saturday morning, the catechumens gather in the evening for a vigil, at which the *traditio orationis* takes place.

Introduction to Origen

Origen

As general introductions to Origen abound,[1] only the briefest
account, sufficient to orientate readers of his work on prayer, is necessary here. Trigg states that in *On Prayer* we have "perhaps the most
representative of Origen's works." The text itself, therefore, provides
the best introduction to Origen. As Trigg goes on to say: "Here we
see Origen as a grammarian, an allegorist, a philosophical theologian in the Platonic tradition, an opponent of heresy, and a Christian of fervent piety."[2] This introduction will touch on each aspect
described here.

We are well informed about Origen's life, since much of the sixth
book of Eusebius' *Ecclesiastical History* is given over to him. Although
Eusebius should not be taken completely uncritically, he had access
to Origen's correspondence, and much other material, through the
library at Caesarea, and had, moreover, been a pupil of Pamphilus,
himself a curator of Origen's library at Caesarea. He was therefore in
a uniquely privileged position to discuss Origen's life. We also have,
moreover, the report by Photius of Pamphilus' *Apology for Origen;*[3]
although most of this work has been lost, Photius' report of the work
is of some use in providing a brief biographical sketch, which enables
us to see that it was the basis for Eusebius' work.

Origen was born around 185 in Alexandria and, having moved
to Caesarea early in the 230s, died either at Tyre or (less reliably

---

[1]Among these, especial mention should be given to the chapter devoted to Origen in John Behr, *The Way to Nicaea* (Crestwood NY: St Vladimir's Seminary Press,
2001), 162–206.

[2]J. W. Trigg, *Origen* (London: SCM, 1985), 157.

[3]Photius *Library* 118.

reported) at Caesarea, around 254. We may therefore see him as an older contemporary of Cyprian. Indeed, in the Decian persecution, during which Cyprian went into hiding, Origen was imprisoned and tortured, treatment which no doubt hastened his death.

His father, Leonides, was beheaded in a persecution early in the third century, from which method of execution we may deduce that he had been a Roman citizen; that Origen was tortured implies that he himself was not, which indicates that his mother had no citizenship. Leonides had already schooled Origen in grammar, which included much of what we would recognize as the study of literature, and in Scripture. After his death, Origen enjoyed the patronage of an Alexandrian lady in whose house he dwelt, together with an Antiochene called Paul. An account is given of Paul's teaching, and of prayer within the house, which indicates that this was some kind of school-household, though, according to Eusebius, Origen would not join in prayer with Paul, on the grounds of Paul's heresy.[4] Soon, however, he started teaching in his own right, after some years abandoning secular teaching and teaching only Christianity, selling his library in return for a small income which would support him whilst teaching. At some point it seems that Origen's school came under the control of the bishop of Alexandria, and was known as the "catechetical school." Nonetheless his fame extended beyond Alexandria, and he travelled to Rome, to Antioch, and to Palestine in order to teach and engage in theological discussion. He continued in this manner until the age of around 40, at which point the same Ambrosius, who is the dedicatee of the work on prayer, was converted from Valentinian beliefs and put his fortune at the disposal of Origen,[5] enabling Origen to begin publication of his writings with the aid of shorthand writers and copyists.

Early in the 230s Origen undertook a journey to Athens, and stayed en route in Caesarea, a city that he had previously visited. On this occasion he was ordained a presbyter by the bishop of Caesarea,

[4]*Ecclesiastical History* (= *EH*) 6.2.13–14.
[5]*EH* 6.18; 6.23.1–2.

Theoctenus, with the consent of Alexander, bishop of Jerusalem, an action that led to a breach with Demetrius, the bishop of Alexandria. On an earlier visit to Caesarea Origen had discoursed in the presence of the bishops, which led to an angry reaction from Demetrius, who held that a layman should not "give homilies" in the presence of a bishop, and recalled Origen to Alexandria.

Origen's ordination at Caesarea thus led to further wrath from Demetrius, which led in turn to his expulsion from Alexandria, the ceding of Origen's school to Heraklas, and Origen's settlement in Caesarea. Beyond this, Demetrius failed to recognize the validity of Origen's ordination. It was at this point that Demetrius made public the fact that Origen had, in his youth, undergone self-castration, using this as an argument for Origen's deposition from the presbyterate.[6] Eusebius states that this was the result of Origen's literal interpretation of Matthew 19.12;[7] if this is so, it is an interpretation which Origen himself subsequently vehemently scorned. The account is puzzling for this reason, but Eusebius is a supporter of Origen, which means that it is unlikely that he would maliciously report something not to Origen's credit. Origen is not the only example of self-castration in Alexandria; Justin records that a Christian had sought permission for surgical castration from the prefect of Egypt, though such permission was refused.[8] There seems to be a common context for this action.[9]

As a result of this expulsion Origen returned to Caesarea and resumed his teaching duties there, apparently with the full blessing of the ecclesiastical authorities, since a number of his homilies are extant from this period. Gregory the Wonderworker was a pupil of Origen at Caesarea, and in his *Address of Thanks* he describes for us Origen's curriculum, which began with logic, proceeded through

[6]*EH* 6.8.4–5.
[7]*EH* 6.8.2.
[8]*First Apology* 29:2–3.
[9]Cf. A. Rousselle, *Porneia: On Desire and the Body in Antiquity*, trans. F. Pheasant (Oxford: Basil Blackwell, 1988).

ethics to the study of philosophy, and finally to the reading of Scripture. This period of his life lasted some twenty years, and ended with Origen's imprisonment and torture in the Decian persecution;[10] although he survived this persecution, he did not survive much longer. It is from this period of his life that *On Prayer* derives. In chapter 23 he is discussing the contents of Gen 3, and states that he has discussed this passage in his commentary on that book. Eusebius tells us that only the first eight books of this commentary were written before Origen left Alexandria, and since Gen 4.15 was discussed in book 13, we may reasonably assume that discussion of the third chapter was in a later book than book 8.[11]

Origen as a teacher was fundamentally an exegete. This is obvious from a reading of the work *On Prayer*, in which Scripture plays the central role as the proof of each proposition proposed, and as the central presupposition of every assertion; indeed, the Lord's Prayer is taken as the prayer par excellence because it is scriptural prayer, and is treated not in any liturgical form but as Scripture cited after the two versions found in the Gospels.[12] Nonetheless Origen read Scripture as a Platonist. Platonist philosophy at the time of Origen had developed into a system and was extensively influenced by the religious preoccupations of neo-Pythagoreanism, but quite apart from its systematic aspects, Platonism supplied the intellectual framework, which both provided the different trains of enquiry pursued by philosophers in antiquity and to an extent dictated the terms in which these enquiries were answered.

[10]*EH* 6.39.4.

[11]See the discussion of E. G. Jay, *Origen's Treatise on Prayer* (London: SPCK, 1954), 72.

[12]F. E. Vokes, "The Lord's Prayer in the First Three Centuries," in F. L. Cross, ed., *Studia Patristica* 10 (TU107; Berlin: Akademie, 1970), 253–260, suggests that the Lord's Prayer comes to sudden prominence in the third century because it is scriptural, and that this is the result of the effective canonization of the Gospels. Silence in the second century may, however, result from the secrecy surrounding this prayer, a secrecy which is discussed in my article "Catechumenate and Contra-Culture: The Social Process of Catechumenate in Third-Century Africa and Its Development," *SVTQ* 47, no.3–4 (2003):289–306.

The fundamental issue for Plato was that of how anything could come to be known, given that we are living in a world that is in a constant state of flux and alteration; it is from Plato's answers to this problem that the rest of the system grew. In response to the problem of knowledge Plato proposed that, whereas what we perceive in this present world is a pale reflection of the knowable reality, there are such realities that are the object of knowledge. So he compares people on earth to those living in a cave, whose vision is that of shadows cast upon a wall, who nonetheless might come to emerge from the cave to see, and know, the real objects outside the cave, in the light of the sun,[13] images of which Origen makes explicit use in *On Prayer* 17.1, in comparing earthly goods received as a result of prayer to shadows of the spiritual realities which are principally granted.

This insight extends not only to objects and ideas, but also to people and to texts. So Origen reads beyond the letter of the scriptural text in order to discern the true meaning that is present behind it. In *On Prayer* this is most obvious at 17.13, where Origen seeks to comprehend the meaning hidden in the precepts of the Mosaic law regarding the intervals at which feasts are to be kept, but more generally he interprets the requests made in prayer by scriptural characters not simply as prayers for earthly requests but as prayers for supernatural blessings. In other words, there is a meaning behind the meaning of the text that immediately presents itself, just as there is a reality behind the raw data received by sense perception. Origen was not the first to apply this exegetical method to Scripture, for it was employed in Alexandria by Philo the Jew in the first century. Moreover, it was a method commonly employed in pagan discussion of Homer, and was employed beyond the narrow confines of strictly Platonic schools. But Origen reflects on the methodology, comparing the senses of Scripture to the way in which a human being is made up of body, soul, and spirit.[14]

---

[13] *Republic* 6.508c–509d and 7.514a–517a.
[14] *On First Principles* 4.1–3.

This tripartite division of the human person perhaps typifies Origen's approach, for whereas the source of the expression is scriptural, Origen's use of the division represents an adaptation of this scriptural phrase to the tripartite division of the human person known to Platonist anthropology.[15] This does not extend simply to seeing the true personality as the soul and not the outward body, but essential to Origen's understanding is the Platonic presupposition that our incorporeal souls are pre-existent spiritual beings that have fallen into the corporeal state. In illustration of this we may note in particular the discussion in *On Prayer* 29 of the manner in which people under temptation may fall to a particular extent, which reflects a fall into the corporeal state through estrangement from the divinity. Thus the whole Incarnation is described in *On Prayer* 23 as a voluntary fall into the body on the part of Jesus, in order to lead us back to the divinity. Indeed the whole life of prayer may be seen in Platonic terms as an ascent of the soul to the divinity from which we are estranged. Eusebius describes Origen's lifestyle in the early years at Alexandria in the terms typical of a philosophical biography of the period, noting Origen's simplicity of dress and diet and the long hours he spent in study. Whereas we may be suspicious of this because of the extent to which it conforms to the expected lifestyle

[15]Cf. M. J. Edwards, *Origen against Plato* (Aldershot: Ashgate, 2002), 87–89, for whom the division is derived solely from I Thessalonians 5:23. This brief phrase would hardly have come to be the centerpiece of an anthropology had it not readily accorded with a philosophical anthropology that already existed. Edwards seeks to deny Platonic influence upon Origen altogether. Although he is right that this aspect of Origen's thought has been overemphasized in the past, with a corresponding failure to recognize Origen's originality, and although his book contains some useful reconsiderations of Origen's position, particularly on the nature of the soul's preexistence, Edwards' denial of Platonism does not in the end convince. He suggests in conclusion that Origen's position vis-à-vis Plato is like that of a modern apologist who must inevitably give attention to Marx and Freud, without actually following either (161). A better analogy would be between Barth and Kierkegaard. Without simply following existentialist agenda, and in a context in which existentialism had come to exhibit great variety and distinctions in detail, Barth, as systematic theologian, laying claim to a reformation heritage of *sola scriptura*, nonetheless cannot be read except from within an existentialist framework, even though Barth's writing often breaks out of the frame.

of a philosopher, the phenomenon of the ascetic philosopher was a real one, and there was a philosophical rationale for the lifestyle which would fit in with Origen's overall philosophical and theological outlook, and so we must assume that there is a degree of truth in this description. The point of the ascetic exercises was to liberate the soul from dependence upon the body in which it found itself.

Whereas these ideas may seem strange and foreign to us, they spoke to people of his day. In a later period Origen came to be considered a heretic, but we must recognize that in his own context he was firmly within an orthodox tradition of thought, and that his fundamental concern was to commend the Christian faith to the intelligentsia of his day. This intelligentsia was strongly influenced by the same Platonism which Origen presupposed; the difference between Origen and his pagan contemporaries was that, first for Origen, Plato simply supplied the intellectual framework by which the sacred text, namely the Bible, made present on earth in the person of Jesus, might come to be understood, whereas for pagan Platonists Plato himself was the sacred text, and second that, for Platonists of a pagan background, the ascent to the divine was something to be undertaken by individual effort, whereas Origen sees that God intends each soul for salvation, and stands ready to supply whatever help is sought in order to attain salvation.

THE PURPOSE AND CHARACTER OF ORIGEN'S TREATISE

Little is known of Christian initiation in Alexandria at the time of Origen. However, the existence of a catechumenate is indubitable, since the catechetical process is referred to several times by Clement,[16] albeit without clarification of the curriculum, and by Origen, who implies that the fundamental purpose of catechesis was the moral

---

[16]E.g. at *Instructor* 1.6.

conversion of the convert.[17] However, no hint here is given of instruction in prayer, in which context a *traditio orationis* might take place. The same is true of the *Canons of Hippolytus*, a reworking of *Apostolic Tradition* deriving from Egypt, albeit not from Alexandria itself. For apart from the material deriving from *Apostolic Tradition*, the canons imply a period of instruction of forty days, and dictate that instruction be given in the Scriptures,[18] but say nothing concerning instruction in prayer. Even though it is hard to imagine that there would be no instruction in prayer, there is thus no evidence of a ritual comparable to the *traditio orationis*. Since, as we have seen, *On Prayer* is a product of Origen's time in Caesarea, we may note that the same was true of Caesarea. However, instruction in the Lord's Prayer is found in the mystagogical catecheses of Cyril of Jerusalem in the context of instruction on the eucharist after baptism, and not prior to baptism, which was the place of the *traditio orationis* in Africa. It may be this practice to which Origen alludes in *On Prayer* 2.4, though this depends on an emendation of the text, at least part of the justification for which is the conformity with the tradition as found in Cyril's writings, and so this cannot be confidently asserted. Finally we may note further evidence of instruction in the Lord's Prayer in the Antiochene tradition through the catechetical homilies of Theodore of Mopsuestia. It is impossible to say with certainty whether this preceded or followed baptism, as the homily on the Lord's Prayer follows those on the creed, and precedes those on the sacraments proper; nonetheless Theodore's statement that the address to "Our Father" states what the candidates "have become"[19] implies a delivery after baptism. Admittedly it has a catechetical context, but we cannot therefore assume that it took place at a formal *traditio orationis* and, in any event, the catechumenate was much altered, due to the different circumstances of Christianity in the period after Nicaea.

[17] *Homily on Jude* 5.
[18] *Canons of Hippolytus* Canon 10 and Canon 12.
[19] *Catechetical Homily* 11.7.

Thus although the *traditio orationis* has been suggested as the basis of Origen's work,[20] not only does the absence of evidence for a ritual moment at which the Lord's Prayer might be explained tend to exclude such an explanation of its contents, the very contents themselves tend to exclude such an origin. For although Origen's work contains a commentary on the Lord's Prayer, it is a commentary of depth and complexity, and prefaced by technical discussion of some very abstruse points such as problems for free will posed by the answering of prayer, which are hardly the material of catechetical lectures but point to a setting in more advanced studies. The length of the treatment of the Lord's Prayer, which is considerably greater than that of Tertullian or Cyprian, likewise tends to point away from a catechetical origin, as the relative absence of the features of the *diatribē*, which is a style of address typical of the schoolroom, points away from a setting in basic instruction.

There are occasional diatribal elements, however, in particular the occasional appearance of imaginary opponents, which points to a locus of instruction, and there is no question, moreover, that the piece is informed by the activities of the Christian schools since we may see that the work bears the particular impress of what, in the ancient world, was known as grammar.

Grammar covered a number of activities, which we would basically recognize as literary criticism, and formed the major part of the school curriculum before specialism either in rhetoric or philosophy, in the early empire becoming increasingly a specialism in its own right. The ancient sources are not in agreement about the precise contents of the grammatical curriculum, but typically would involve the study of vocabulary, pronunciation, explanation of the contents of a text, and lexicology, as well as the critique of style. Thus the discussion of the distinction between *proseuchē* (vow) and *euchē* (prayer) which emerges from the lexical search for the word "prayer" in Scripture with which the work begins is, according to Gessel,

---

[20]E.g. by A. Hamman, *La prière* II (Tournai: Desclée, 1959), 297.

undertaken in the manner of an Alexandrian grammarian.[21] The same may be said of the discussion of the word "name" at 24.2 in the commentary on the petition that God's name be hallowed, and most especially of the lengthy discussion of the meaning of the Greek word here translated as "supersubstantial" which, as Origen notes, does not otherwise appear in Greek literature. Indeed, the commentary on the Lord's Prayer begins by noting the two different versions in which the Gospels transmit the prayer, rather than assuming a single version which the audience is to learn, which implies that the prayer is being read as Scripture rather than being taught to an audience of catechumens, but is also indicative of the approach of a grammarian concerned to establish the text on which comment is to be given. Gessel also suggests that the heap of citations at *On Prayer* 27 is indicative of a school tradition,[22] and we may finally note Origen's observation at 14.4 of an obelus in the text of Tobit employed among Jews. Likewise speaking of its intellectual tone, in keeping with the Alexandrian provenance of its author, is the fairly strict Atticism of the vocabulary and periodic construction of the piece.[23] The work may, therefore, reflect the discourse that might have taken place in the advanced section of the Alexandrian school and in Origen's academy at Caesarea.

With regard to its purpose in that setting we may accept with Gessel that the work is broadly symbouleutic in purpose, that it is intended to win the audience over to the practice of prayer in accordance with scriptural examples and precepts, and in particular to those of the Lord. The structure, however, has baffled commentators.[24] Nonetheless if we take the formal canons of the construction

---

[21]W. Gessel, *Die Theologie des Gebets nach "De Oratione" von Origenes* (Munich: Schöningh, 1975), 45, with reference to *On Prayer* 3–4.

[22]Gessel, *Theologie*, 62.

[23]For a discussion see Gessel, *Theologie*, 17–35.

[24]E.g., E. von der Goltz, *Das Gebet in der ältesten Christenheit* (Leipzig: Hinrichs, 1901), 267: "In the introduction and sequence of ideas, repetitions and minor obscurities are not lacking." This is quoted with approval by R. L. Simpson, *The Interpretation of Prayer in the Early Church* (Philadelphia: Westminster, 1965), 33. Likewise Trigg

of ancient discourse seriously, and seek a *propositio*, the point at which an author states his purpose, we may see that Origen sets out his purpose near the beginning of the work.

> I am persuaded, insofar as our weakness might tell, that one of the impossible things is to treat the whole subject of prayer accurately and reverently, discussing the manner in which one should pray, and what one should say to God in prayer, and what occasions, and how many occasions, are most fitting for prayer . . . It is an obligation on us not only to pray, but also to pray as we ought, and to pray for what we ought. For if we know the things for which we ought to pray, this is inadequate, unless we also grasp the manner in which we ought to pray. But what benefit is it to us if we know how we should pray if we do not know what we ought to request.

The subjects are, therefore, the manner in which we should pray and the intent with which we should make that prayer. Thus the first part of the work is concerned with disposition, and the attitude with which we should set ourselves to the task of prayer, which includes a right attitude to those things which we should ask, and the second with the manner in which we should pray. The manner, as Origen states, includes the words which we should use in prayer, namely the Lord's Prayer, which is the means of introducing the commentary on the text, and the reason why advice about posture and place follow the commentary, since these, like the words which we use, concern the manner in which we should pray.

Quintilian states that every speech (*oratio*) is of necessity constructed of what is to be expressed, and the means of the expression.[25] Here he is employing the distinction widespread in ancient

states: "Although reasonably precise and clear, Origen's treatise is not perfectly well organised" (*Origen*, 158).

[25]"Ex iis, quae significantur, aut et iis, quae significant." Quintilian *Beginning Public Speaking* 3.5.1.

rhetoric between the content of a literary work (*heuresis*), and the style in which it is expressed (*lexis*).[26] Should this insight be applied to Origen's work, we may see that he treats prayer in the same way, dealing in the first instance with the subject of prayer, namely its content and object, and going on, in his commentary on the Lord's Prayer, to deal with the words which should be employed in praying.

A number of things make this pattern hard to discern, chief among which are the explorations of grammar, such as the distinction made between *euchē* and *proseuchē* with its accompanying discussion, and the enumeration of the different kinds of prayer distinguished in Paul's writings. According to Dionysius Thrax, the clarification of these preliminary matters follows on from an initial reading of a text, and precedes the clarification of the meaning of any text.[27] Thus these technical discussions of the meaning of the terms used precede the discussion of prayer proper. They also intervene into the discussion such as the discussion of the definition of "name" in the commentary on the petition "let your name be hallowed," and the exploration of the meaning of "supersubstantial." But his forays into the grammar of Scripture demonstrate a proper concern for *lexis*, which is of necessity the means by which the commentator uncovers the content of the work. Second, again in a manner reminiscent of a grammarian, Origen proves each point with reference to Scripture. Sometimes the citations are so long, and need commentary of themselves, that it is easy to lose track of the point that is being made. Finally, especially in the earlier part of the work, in which objections to the efficacy of prayer are cleared out of the way, the philosophical arguments about such matters as the compatibility of providence and free will, whilst readily comprehensible to an ancient audience trained in philosophy, seem abstruse and irrelevant to a modern audience.

But Origen's intent, as an intellectual of the third century, is to lead an audience that shared his background and presuppositions

[26]See, for instance, Lucian *How to Write History* 47–48.
[27]Dionysius Thrax *On the Art of Grammar* 1.

into the mysteries of a life of prayer. His school was a school of salvation, and his purpose is to lead his hearers to salvation in a manner that was as accessible and familiar to them. As such, as Eusebius states, and as Origen himself states his aim in a defense of his actions produced whilst under attack by Demetrius, he led many of the cultured to the church, and away from the heresies which had superficial attraction to those who held the general assumption of the educated classes. If we can get beyond what is foreign to us, then Origen's message that this life is a preparation for the glory that is to come in the providence of God, and that prayer is the means by which we can lay claim to this providence, is a message for us as well as for his first audience.

Appendix I: The hours of prayer according to Origen

At *On Prayer* 12.2 we read, with regard to the hours of prayer, "this should not be performed less than three times each day." He subsequently states: "Indeed, we should acknowledge that the night is not without a fitting occasion of prayer."

The second of these three occasions of prayer during the day is explicitly stated to be noon. It is therefore possible that this is a reference to the third, sixth, and ninth hours, the day hours known to Tertullian and Cyprian,[28] though alternative understandings are proposed by Jay and Bradshaw. For Jay the three are night, noon, and evening,[29] but Bradshaw suggests that prayer at night is separate and additional to the three hours of prayer in the day since it is mentioned additionally in the same chapter. He then refers to the

[28]So C. W. Dugmore, *The Influence of the Synagogue upon the Divine Office*, 2nd ed. (Westminster: Faith Press, 1964), 67–68; Joan Hazelden Walker, "Terce, Sext and None: An Apostolic Custom?" in F. L. Cross, ed., *Studia patristica* 5 (TU 80; Berlin: Akademie, 1962), 206–212, at 209; L. E. Phillips, "Daily Prayer in the *Apostolic Tradition* of Hippolytus," *JTS* n.s. 40 (1989): 390–400 at 396.

[29]Jay, *Origen's Treatise*, 115–116 n. 3.

evidence of Clement; Clement speaks at one point of "prayer on rising in the morning, and in the middle of the day, . . ."[30] and so Bradshaw concludes that two of these hours are those to which Origen refers, and that the third must therefore be prayer in the evening, to which Clement refers elsewhere alongside prayer during the night, and which is indicated by Origen's citation of the psalm verse "the lifting up of my hands as an evening sacrifice."[31]

Bradshaw's conclusions here are disputed by Phillips, who suggests that this "evening prayer" might take place at the ninth hour, on the grounds that the ninth hour, as Origen might well have been aware, was that at which the sacrifice was offered in the Temple.[32] He goes on from there to suggest that the morning prayer to which Origen refers might take place at the third hour, and thus that the three hours are the third, sixth, and ninth hour. This is possible, for it does seem that some at Alexandria had conformed prayer at morning, noon, and evening to the pattern of the third, sixth, and ninth hours,[33] but Phillips' argument here is far from compelling, even though Bradshaw concedes the point.[34] Origen is not concerned to align the hour of prayer with that of sacrifice but to find a scriptural warrant for the practice of praying in the evening.

Origen thus commends a practice of praying in the morning, at midday, and in the evening, with additional prayer at midnight. This is a pattern derived from Judaism. Given the Caesarean provenance of the work, it is possible that this is a pattern current in Palestine, which had survived from the first century until the third.[35]

[30] *Stromata* 7.12.

[31] P. F. Bradshaw, *Daily Prayer in the Early Church* (London: SPCK, 1981), 49.

[32] Phillips, "Daily Prayer," 396.

[33] This would explain the statement of Clement at *Stromata* 7.7 that some pray at these times.

[34] P. F. Bradshaw, *The Search for the Origins of Christian Worship* (London: SPCK, 2002), 176.

[35] For further discussion of the hours of prayer in the early churches see my "Prayer Five Times in the Day and at Midnight: Two Apostolic Customs!" *Studia Liturgica*, 33 (2003): 1–19.

Appendix II: The contents of Origen's treatise

The following brief analysis is offered as orientation to the reader who may lose direction in the length and complexity of Origen's treatise amidst the many proofs and subsidiary discussions. It is meant only as a guide, and not as an exhaustive analysis of the contents of the treatise.

1: Dedication

2: Proposition
> 3–7: Preliminary matters
> 3–4: Lexical examination of words for prayer in Scripture
> 5–7: Philosophical objections to prayer

8–33: Praying as we ought and for what we ought
> 8–13: The disposition toward prayer
> 14–15: To whom we should pray
> 16–17: For what we should pray
> 18–21: The Lord's Prayer as the prayer that guides us aright in disposition
> 22–23: The Lord's Prayer as the prayer that guides us aright in direction
> 24–30: The Lord's Prayer as the prayer that guides us aright in content
> 31–32: The manner in which we should pray
> 33: The parts from which any prayer should be constructed

34: Conclusion

Origen: *On Prayer*

1

Matters which are so immense and so beyond humanity, so sur-
passing and exceeding our perishable nature that they are impossible for those of a rational and mortal class to comprehend, have, in
the vast and immeasurable grace which is poured from God toward
humanity, become, by the will of God, comprehensible through
Jesus Christ, the minister of boundless grace to us, and through the
collaborating Spirit. Although it is impossible for human nature to
obtain the wisdom by which all things have been established (for,
according to David, God made all things "in wisdom" [Ps 103.24]),
it becomes possible, rather than impossible, through our Lord Jesus
Christ, "who was made our wisdom from God and righteousness
and sanctification and redemption" (1 Cor 1.30). "For what does a
human know of the will of God? Or who shall conceive of what the
Lord wills since the considerations of mortals are fearful and our
purposes are prone to fail? For a corruptible body weighs down the
soul, and the earthly dwelling-place burdens a mind that ponders
many things. We hardly forecast earthly matters, so who can trace
out whatever is in heaven?" (Wis 9.13–16) Indeed, who would not say
that it is impossible for a human being to trace out "whatever is in
heaven"? Yet by the overflowing grace of God this impossible thing
becomes at the same time possible. For he who was caught up to the
third heaven surely traced out whatever was in the three heavens
through having heard unutterable utterances, which were not per-
mitted for a person to speak (cf. 2 Cor 12.4). Who can say that it is
possible for a human to know the mind of the Lord? (cf. 1 Cor 2.16)
But God grants even this through Christ . . .[1] the will of their Lord,

---

[1]A gap of three lines follows here. It is possible that Origen cited Jn 14.15 (which
concerns Christ's making known to his disciples what he had heard from the Father).

when he teaches them the will of the Lord that he desires to become a friend to those of whom he was formerly a master. But just as nobody knows a person's affairs apart from the human spirit that is in him, so nobody knows what is of God apart from the Spirit of God (1 Cor 2.11). Now if no one knows what is of God apart from the Spirit of God it is impossible that a human might know what is of God. Yet take good note how it becomes possible indeed: "Yet we," he says, "did not receive the spirit of the world but the Spirit which is from God, so that we might know whatever is freely granted us by God; we speak of these matters not in words taught by human wisdom but in those taught by the Spirit" (1 Cor 2.12–13).

2

1   But it seems, most pious and industrious Ambrosius and most discreet and manly Tatiana (for whom, I profess, womanly ways have been left behind in the manner in which Sarah previously left them behind),[2] that you should wonder, when the subject set before us is prayer, why the preface has spoken of the things which, impossible for humanity, are made possible through the grace of God. I am persuaded, insofar as our weakness might tell, that one of the impossible things is to treat the whole subject of prayer accurately and reverently, discussing the manner in which one should pray, and what one should say to God in prayer, and what occasions, and how many occasions, are most fitting for prayer ... [Note that Paul,][3] who was cautious because of the abundance of his revelations lest anyone should rate him more highly than what he sees or hears from him (2 Cor 12.6–7), admits that he knows not how to pray as he should. For, he says, we ought to pray, but we do not know the way we ought to pray (Rom 8.26). It is an obligation on us not only to pray, but also

[2]A reference to Gen 18.11, implying that Tatiana, in her mature years, has committed herself to chastity.

[3]There is a gap of several lines in the manuscript; the words in brackets beginning the first sentence after the gap are editorial.

to pray as we ought, and to pray for what we ought. For if we know the things for which we ought to pray this is inadequate, unless we also grasp the manner in which we ought to pray. But what benefit is it to us if we know how we should pray if we do not know what we ought to request.

2   Of these two matters one, I speak of praying for what we ought, concerns the words of the prayer; the other, the manner in which we ought to pray, concerns the disposition of the one who prays. As examples of that for which we ought to pray we have, "Ask for great things, and minor matters will be provided for you,"[4] and "Ask for heavenly things, and mundane things will be provided for you" (Mt 6.33), and "Pray for those who abuse you" (Mt 5.44), and "Pray that the Lord of the harvest should send laborers into his harvest" (Mt 9.38), and "Pray that you be not put to the test" (Lk 22.40), and "Pray that your flight should not be in the winter or on a Sabbath" (Mt 24.20), and "Do not babble when you pray" (Mt 6.7), and passages similar to these. As regards the manner in which we should pray we have, "I desire therefore that men should pray in every place, lifting up holy hands without anger and dissension. In like manner women should array themselves in decency and in simplicity, adorning themselves with modesty and discretion, as is fitting to women who proclaim their devotion to God in good works, not with braided hair, or in gold or pearls or expensive clothes" (1 Tim 2.8–10). Also instructive for the manner in which we should pray is the passage: "If you are offering your gift at the altar, and there recall that your brother has something against you, leave the gift there before the altar and go straightaway to be reconciled with your brother, and then come and offer your gift" (Mt 5.23–24). For what greater gift for God from a rational creature can there be than the sending up of fragrant speech in prayer, offered from a conscience

---

[4]Although this saying is also quoted by Origen at *Against Celsus* 7.726, and by Clement at *Stromata* 1.24, it does not appear in the Scriptures. It is possible that it is an Alexandrian addition to Mt 6.33 as Origen cites it at 14.1 below together with Mt 6.33.

devoid of the taint of sin? Further with regard to the manner in which we should pray is: "Do not separate from one another, unless by agreement for a set period so that you may concentrate on prayer, and then come together again, so that Satan is not able to rejoice over your incontinence" (1 Cor 7.5). For the ability to pray as we should is diminished unless the task which is the mystery of marriage (concerning which it is fitting that we should keep silence) be performed more reverently and deliberately and less passionately. For the agreement to which reference is made in this passage dissipates the discord of passion and destroys incontinence, so preventing Satan from malicious rejoicing. Further instructive concerning the manner in which we should pray is: "If you are standing at prayer, forgive whatever you hold against anybody" (Mk 11.25) and that from Paul, also setting forth the manner in which we should pray: "Every man who prays or prophesies with his head covered brings shame upon his head, and any woman who prays or prophesies with her head uncovered brings shame upon her head" (1 Cor 11.4–5).

3   But Paul, who is knowledgeable of all these texts, and could cite many more from the law and the prophets and from their fulfillment in the Gospel, stating each with great subtlety, sees, not only due to the moderation of his nature but also in his honesty, that after all this so much is lacking with regard to knowledge of the manner in which we ought to pray. "We do not know the manner in which we should pray for things for which we ought to pray" (Rom 8.26). And in addition he states here the source from which the deficiency is to be made up should anybody who is ignorant be prepared and made worthy to have what is lacking made good: "The Spirit himself, with unutterable groanings, makes intercession with God. And the one who searches out the hearts knows what the mind of the Spirit is, because his intercession with God on behalf of the saints is in accordance with God" (Rom 8.26–7). The Spirit which, in the hearts of the blessed, cries out "Abba, Father" (Gal 4.6), knows in his solicitude that the groanings in this tent can only weigh down those who have fallen or wandered, and so "with unutterable groanings makes

intercession with God," taking our groanings upon himself in great love for humanity and in his sympathy. In the wisdom which is in him, as he sees that our soul is humbled to dust (Ps 43.26) and enclosed in the body of our humiliation (Phil 3.21), so he makes intercession for us with God; not with mundane groanings but with those which are "unutterable," similar to those unspeakable words which a human is not to utter (2 Cor 12.4). This Spirit, not content simply to intercede with God, intensifies his pleading, does more, I think, than intercede, for those such as Paul who more than conquer (for he says: "But in all these things we do more than conquer" [Rom 8.37]). It would seem that he simply intercedes for those who conquer, and more than intercedes for those who "more than conquer," and does not intercede at all for those who are conquered.

4   Akin to the passage concerning what we should pray, "We do not know the manner in which we should pray but the Spirit intercedes with God with unutterable groanings," is "I will pray in the Spirit, and I will pray in the mind also. I will sing out in the Spirit and I will sing out in the mind also" (1 Cor 14.15). For our mind cannot pray unless the Spirit pray first, as it were within earshot, just as it cannot sing out with rhythm and melody and tempo and harmony, hymning the Father in Christ, unless the Spirit which searches all things, even the depths of God, first gives praise and hymns him whose depths he has searched out and, as he is able, comprehended. I think that it was the realization of the extent to which human weakness falls short of the manner in which we should pray, recognized especially when he heard the words of great insight expressed by the Savior in his prayer to the Father, that caused one of the disciples of Jesus to say to the Lord when he ceased from prayer: "Lord, teach us to pray, just as John taught his disciples"(Lk 11.1). The whole context of this passage is as follows: "It happened that, when he was praying in a certain place, one of his disciples said to him when he ceased: 'Lord, teach us to pray, just as John taught his disciples to pray.' "[5]

---

[5]There is a gap of several lines here. As the next paragraph follows on in terms of sense, it is possible that the passage continued with the citation of Luke.

Is it indeed to be supposed that a man who had been nurtured in the instruction of the law, who listened to the words of the prophets, who did not desert the synagogue, had absolutely no knowledge of prayer until he saw the Lord praying in a certain place?

This is foolish talk! For he prayed according to the customs of the Jews, and saw that he was in need of a greater knowledge on the subject of prayer. And what did John teach his disciples concerning prayer when they came to him to be baptized from Jerusalem and all Judaea and the surrounding countryside (Mt 3.5) unless he perceived something concerning prayer, insofar as he was "beyond being a prophet" (Mt 11.9) which, it is likely, he would deliver not to all who were being baptized but secretly to those who were being trained in addition to baptism.[6]

5   Such prayers are recorded, which are truly spiritual and are filled with unutterable and wonderful teaching, since the Spirit prays in the hearts of the saints. In the first book of Kingdoms is that of Hannah (in part, for the whole was not committed to writing, since she was "speaking in her heart" when she "persisted in prayer before the Lord" [1 Kg 1.12–13]), and among the psalms the sixteenth Psalm is entitled "A prayer of David" and the eighty-ninth "A prayer from Moses, a man of God," and the hundred and first "A prayer from a poor man when he is weary and pours forth his supplication before the Lord." Since they are truly prayers that are spoken in the Spirit, such prayers are also filled with the teaching and the wisdom of God. Thus one might say concerning the matters proclaimed within them: "Who is wise, yet understands these things. And who is understanding and recognizes them?" (Hos 14.9).

[6]The text reads "those being trained *for* baptism." The text is emended, in line with Anglus, as otherwise the statement that only some of those who were baptized were given instruction would be strange to say the least. As emended, the text coheres with the practice of Cyril of Jerusalem (it is to be noted that Jerusalem, in the third century, was a suffragan see of Caesarea and might be expected to follow the same practice), and probably also with the practice of Theodore of Mopsuestia, of providing mystagogical catechesis after baptism, in the course of which the Lord's Prayer was explained. It is also to be noted that there is a hint here of a *disciplina arcani* surrounding the subject of prayer.

6   Since the discussion of prayer is such a task that the illumination of the Father is needed, as well as the teaching of the firstborn Word and the inner working of the Spirit, so that it is possible to think and to speak worthily on such a topic, as a man (for of myself I do not claim capacity for prayer) I am entreating the Spirit before I begin to discuss prayer, so that a discourse which is full and spiritual might be granted to us, and that the prayers which are recorded in the Gospels may be clarified.

Now we should begin the discourse on prayer . . .[7]

3

1   The first mention of the word "prayer" (*euchē*) which I have been able to find is that used when Jacob, in flight from the anger of his brother Esau, was departing into Mesopotamia at the suggestion of Isaac and Rebecca. The passage reads as follows: "And Jacob vowed a vow saying: 'If the Lord God is with me and keeps me safe on this road which now I am traveling, and gives me bread to eat and clothing to wear and brings me safely back to my father's house, then the Lord will be my God, and this stone, which I have set up as a pillar, shall be the house of God for me, and I shall make return of a tenth of all that he should grant me'" (Gen 28.20–22).[8]

2   Here, moreover, it is to be observed that the word "prayer" (*euchē*) frequently differs in meaning from "intercession," (*proseuchē*) when it comes to refer to somebody who promises with a vow to do certain things should he obtain certain other things from God.[9] The term is employed, however, in the sense with which it is customarily used by ourselves. So in Exodus we find it employed

---

[7]There is a gap of one and one-third lines in the manuscript here. Some clarification of the purpose of the first part of the discourse would have followed.

[8]There is a gap in the text here. It is possible that another usage of the term "prayer" was found here.

[9]The point here, which is impossible to convey in translation, is that *euchē*, and its related verb, can be both "vow" and "pray." In examining the uses of the term in Scripture, Origen is obliged to clarify which meaning is intended in each instance.

thus after the plague of frogs, which was the second in order of the ten:[10] "Pharaoh called Moses and Aaron and said to them: 'Pray for me to the Lord, and let him remove the frogs from me and from my people. And I will release the people so that they might sacrifice to the Lord'" (Ex 8.8). And should anyone be unpersuaded that that Pharaoh's use of the term "pray" (*euxasthe*) signifies something other than the former use of the term "prayer" (*euchē*) and has its customary usage, let them observe what follows. It states thus: "Moses said to Pharaoh: 'Set the time for me at which I should pray (*euxomai*) for you and for your officers and for your people, for the removal of the frogs from you, and from your people and from your homes, that they should remain only in the river'" (Ex 8.8).

3   We may observe in the case of the lice, the third plague, that Pharaoh neither asks that prayer be made, nor does Moses pray. In the case of the flies, which was the fourth, he says: "Pray for me to the Lord." And then Moses said: "I shall go away from you and I shall pray to God, and the flies shall depart from Pharaoh and his officers and his people tomorrow." And, a little further on: "Moses went away from Pharaoh and prayed to God" (Ex 8.28–30). Once again, in the case of the fifth and sixth plagues, neither did Pharaoh ask that prayer be made, nor did Moses pray. In the case of the seventh, "Pharaoh sent, and called Moses and Aaron, and said to them: 'Now I have sinned. The Lord is just, but I and my people are impious. Pray, therefore, to the Lord that the thundering voice of God, and the hail, and the fire, might cease'" (Ex 9.27–28). And a little further on: "Moses went away from Pharaoh, outside the city, and stretched out his hands to the Lord and the thundering ceased" (Ex 9.33). We may better enquire at another time why it does not say "And he prayed" as it did before, but "He stretched out his hands to the Lord." And in the case of the eighth plague Pharaoh said: "'Pray to the Lord your God, and let him take this death away from me.' And Moses went away from Pharaoh and prayed to God" (Ex 10.17–18).

[10]There is a short gap in the text here. It is impossible to guess what might have been found here.

4   We noted that the word "prayer" (*euchē*) is frequently employed
other than as is usual, as in the passage about Jacob, but also in
Leviticus: "The Lord spoke to Moses saying: 'Speak to the children
of Israel, and say to them: "Should anyone make a vow (*euchē*) to pay
to the Lord the price of his life, the price of a male aged from twenty
to sixty shall be valued at fifty didrachmas of silver according to the
sacred weight"'" (Lev 27.1–3) and in Numbers: "And the Lord spoke
to Moses saying: 'Speak to the children of Israel and say to them:
"Should anyone, man or woman, make a mighty vow (*euchē*) to dedicate themselves to the Lord in purity they shall purify themselves
from wine and strong drink"'" (Num 6.1–3), and what follows concerning the one called a Nazirite. Then, a little later, "And he shall
sanctify his head on that day on which he is dedicated to the Lord,
for the period of the vow" (Num 6.5). And again, a little later: "This
is the law of the one who makes a vow, on the day on which he com-
pletes the period of his vow." And again a little later: "And after that,
the one who has made a vow shall drink wine. This is the law of the
one who makes a vow: if he should vow a gift to the Lord as his vow,
apart from whatever his hand may find in keeping with his vow, he
should make his vow in accordance with the law of purity" (Num
6.20–21). And toward the end of Numbers: "And Moses spoke to the
leaders of the tribes of the children of Israel, saying: 'This is the thing
which the Lord has decreed. Should anyone vow a vow to the Lord,
or swear an oath with a bond, or swear upon his life, he shall not go
back on his word. He shall perform whatever issued from his mouth.
If a woman vows a vow to the Lord or, in her youth, swears an oath
in her father's house, and her father hears her vows and her oaths
which she has made upon her life, and her father keeps his silence,
all her vows shall stand, and all the oaths which she swore upon her
life shall remain binding upon her'" (Num 30.1–4). And following
this there is further legislation with regard to a woman like this. It is
in the sense that it is written among the Proverbs . . . [11] "For a man to

---

[11] There is a gap of two lines here. One suggestion is that Origen quoted Prov
7.14 and 19.13: "I have a peace offering; today I pay my vows" and "A foolish son is a

dedicate anything of his hastily is a snare. For a change of mind may
follow the vow" (Prov 20.25). And in Ecclesiastes: "It is better to
make no vow than to make a vow and not to fulfill it" (Eccl 5.5). And
in the Acts of the Apostles: "We have four men who have a vow upon
themselves" (Acts 21.23).

4

1   It did not seem unreasonable to me first of all to determine that,
according to the Scriptures, prayer (*euchē*) has a double significa-
tion. It is similar with regard to intercession (*proseuchē*). This word
also is frequently employed in the sense with which it is common
and customary for us, as well as in accordance with the customary
way in which it might mean a vow. So it is said of Hannah in the first
book of Kingdoms: "And Eli the priest was sitting on a seat by the
doorway of the Temple of the Lord. And her soul was embittered and
she vowed (*prosēuxato*) to the Lord and wept despondently. And she
vowed a vow (*euchē*) and said: 'Lord of hosts, if indeed you will look
upon your servant's affliction and give the seed of a man to your servant, I shall hand him over to the Lord as a gift for all the days of his
life, and no razor shall come upon his head'" (1 Kg 1.9–11).

2   However, it is not implausible to suggest, paying attention to the
words "she interceded with (*prosēuxato*) the Lord" and "she vowed
a vow (*euchē*)," the possibility that here that she did both things,
namely "interceded with" (*prosēuxato*) the Lord" and "vowed a vow,"
and that the word "interceded with" (*prosēuxato*) is used in the sense
that is customary among us whereas "vowed a vow" is employed
with the meaning that it has in Leviticus and Numbers. For "I shall
hand him over to the Lord as a gift for all the days of his life, and no
razor shall come upon his head" is not properly a plea but it is a vow,
of the kind which Jephthah vowed in the passage: "And Jephthah
vowed a vow to the Lord and said: 'If you deliver the children of

shame to his father; his vows are impure from the hire of a prostitute." The word
"snare" here is editorial.

Ammon into my hand as a gift, then whatever comes out of the doors of my house to meet me upon my return in peace from the children of Ammon shall be the Lord's, and I will offer it up as a whole burnt offering' " (Judg 11.30–31).

5

1   If, as you have demanded, I should next set forth the objections made by whose who assert that nothing comes about as a result of prayer and allege therefore that prayer is superfluous, then I shall not hesitate to do this as far as I am able, now using the term "prayer" in its more common and simple sense.

. . .[12] The argument is poor, and has failed to find eminent supporters. Among those who accept providence and set God over the universe there is none who has no belief in prayer. This is the teaching of those who are entirely atheistic and who deny the existence of God or who admit the name of God but deny his providence. Already the opposing power, desiring to dress the name of Christ and the teaching of the Son of God with the most impious of teachings, has managed to persuade some people that they should not pray. The supporters of this opinion are those who have done away altogether with the things of sense, and who have no use either for baptism or for the eucharist,[13] and who accuse the Scriptures of not intending prayer but teaching that something else entirely is signified in that word.

2   The arguments of those who reject prayer whilst accepting that there is a God set over the universe and assert the existence of providence, for I have no intention of discussing the assertions

---

[12]There is a gap of around two lines here.

[13]Although there is a tale told by Theodoret at *Compendium* 1.25 of an aging Marcionite who despaired because of his inability to celebrate the mysteries without the goods of the creator, and although Irenaeus (*Against the Heresies* 4.18.4) charges that Gnostics cannot consistently offer the gifts of a corrupt creation (as they would see it) there is no evidence beyond this that any group actually abandoned the use of the sacraments on these grounds.

of those who deny God or providence altogether, might be as follow.[14]

God knows all things before they come to be, and nothing that occurs becomes known to him for the first time only when it occurs. So what point is there in sending up prayer to one who knows our needs before we pray? For the heavenly Father knows our needs even before we ask him (cf. Mt 6.8). It is reasonable to suppose that the Father and maker of all that is, who loves all that is and hates nothing that he has made (Wis 11.24), should have concern for the welfare of each of us, without regard to prayer, like a father who provides for and looks after his little children without waiting for them to ask, since they are entirely incapable of asking or because, out of ignorance, they often want the opposite of whatever is to their profit and advantage. As human beings we fall further short of God than the smallest children fall short of their parents' understanding.

3   It is likely that God not only has foreknowledge of what is going to happen but also predisposes it. And nothing happens contrary to his predisposition. So, if anyone should pray that the sun rise, he would be considered a half-wit, for asking that something should happen which would occur quite apart from his prayer. In the same way a man would be considered foolish if he should think that through his prayer he had brought something about which would have happened even had he never prayed at all. Again, just as it would be the height of madness should anyone, being annoyed and scorched by the sun in the summer solstice, imagine that he might transfer the sun to the spring signs in order to enjoy a temperate breeze, so it would be the height of folly should anyone imagine that, through praying, he might avoid the misfortunes which meet the human race as a matter of necessity.

4   If, moreover, "from birth are sinners estranged" (Ps 57.4) while the righteous one is set apart "from his mother's womb" (Gal 1.15) and "whilst they are yet unborn and have done nothing of good or

---

[14]Clement, in *Stromata* 7.7, refers to those who follow Prodicus in denying the necessity of prayer. This could be the group whose arguments Origen is discussing.

evil, so that the purpose of God's choice should remain based not on works but on the grace of the one who calls, it is said, 'the elder shall serve the younger' " (Rom 9.11–12), it is vain to ask for the remission of sins or to ask to receive the Spirit of strength so that Christ might enable us to be strong in all things (Phil 4.13). For if we are sinners we are "estranged from birth." Yet if we are set apart "from our mothers' womb" the best of things will come our way without our praying. For what prayer did Jacob offer before he was born so that it might be said that he be set over Esau and that his brother serve him? And what impiety did Esau commit so that he should be hated before he was born? (cf. Gen 25.23) And why should Moses pray if, as the eighty-ninth Psalm records,[15] God is his "refuge before the mountains were settled, and the earth or the world was formed" (Ps 89.1–2).

5   But[16] in the letter to the Ephesians it is recorded that the Father chose all those who are to be saved in Christ, choosing them in him "before the foundation of the world that they should be holy and blameless before him, foreordaining them for adoption by himself through Christ" (Eph 1.4–5). Therefore somebody is either chosen before the foundation of the world, and it is impossible for him to fall away from this choice, in which case there is no need of prayer, or else he is not chosen and is not foreordained, in which case his prayer is vain for, even should he pray ten thousand times, he will not be heard. For those whom God knew in advance he foreordained to be conformed to the likeness of the glory of his Son. "Those whom he foreordained he also called, and those whom he called he made just, and those whom he made just he also glorified" (Rom 8.29–30). For why does Josiah labor and why, when he prays, is he anxious as to whether or not he will be heard, when he was named many generations before in prophecy, and what he would do was foretold, not only being foreknown but foretold in the presence of many?[17] And

---

[15]The Psalm is attributed to Moses.
[16]The hiatus here may be explained by a gap in the manuscript of about a line and a half.
[17]Cf. 4 Kg 22–23 with reference to the prophecy of 3 Kg 13.2.

why does Judas pray when his prayer is accounted as a sin, since it was announced in advance in the times of David that he should lose his office, and that another would take it from him?[18] Hence it seems that, since God is unchangeable and understands all things before-hand, and is steadfast in his pre-arranged purpose, it would be absurd to think that his disposition might be altered by prayer or to intercede as though he was not predetermined but awaited each individual's prayer, as though he would arrange whatever is proper for the one who prays, ordering at that time whatever would seem to be right and approved, as though he had not envisaged this in advance.

6   At this point let me lay out the very words that you set down when you wrote to me. They are as follow: "Firstly, if God has fore-knowledge of what is to come about, and this will occur of necessity, then prayer is pointless. Secondly: if all things occur through the will of God, and his decrees are fixed, and if nothing which he wills can be altered, prayer is pointless." The following propositions are pre-sented which, I think, are useful in solving the difficulties that lead to unwillingness to pray.

6

1   Some moving objects have the cause of their motion externally, such as lifeless objects that are kept together by their constitution. Similarly there are some objects that, whilst they are moved by nature and inner life, are not moving in this manner when they are treated in the same way as objects that are kept together by their con-stitution. For instance, stones dug out of a quarry, or branches cut away, which have lost the ability to grow, are kept together solely by their constitution and have the cause of their motion externally. The carcasses of animals, and portable plants, when they are being relo-cated by somebody, are not relocating as animals and plants but after

18Acts 1.20, citing Ps 108.8.

the same fashion as stones and branches that have lost the ability to grow. Although even these things may be said to be changing, as all decaying bodies are in a state of alteration, their change is the kind of change that is consequent on decay. Beside these there is a second class of moving objects that are moved by their innate nature or inner life. These things are said to be moved "*of* themselves" by those who are most precise in their use of words. A third kind of movement is that which is in animals, which is called movement "*from* itself." And I consider that movement of rational beings is "movement *through* oneself." If we were to remove motion "from itself" from an animal we could no longer consider it to be an animal, but it would be like a plant, moving solely by virtue of growing, or a stone that is being carried by an external agency. But if the movement of any thing is consequent on its own volition then it is moved "through itself" and of necessity must be considered rational.[19]

2 Therefore those who would have it that nothing is in our power are obliged to admit something foolish, first that we are not animals and secondly that we are not rational, but that whatever we think that we are doing ourselves we are doing not through ourselves at all but through the movement of some external agent. Let anyone consider their own experience; can he see a way to saying honestly that he does not himself intend, does not himself eat, does not himself walk, does not himself assent to and accept some assertions and does not dissent from others as being false. Just as there are some assertions to which it is impossible to assent, even though they be demonstrated with ten thousand proofs, and be stated with plausible reasons, so it is impossible to assent to any statement of human affairs which leaves no place for our free will. For who would admit that nothing is comprehensible, who lives in complete suspension of judgement? Who

---

[19]The distinctions between different kinds of movement originate in the *Phaedrus*. Also taken for granted in this discussion are the Aristotelian ideas, taken up by the Stoics, that any change is a kind of movement, and that any change or movement has a cause; the argument concerning free will here was first developed by Carneades, a follower of Aristotle in the second century BCE. We may compare *On First Principles* 3.1.2 and Clement of Alexandria *Stromata* 2.20.

receives a sense perception of a domestic doing wrong holds off from punishing the servant? Who does not hold culpable a son who fails in his duty to his parents? Who does not blame and censure an adulteress as doing a shameful thing? The truth forces and obliges us impulsively to ascribe praise and blame in spite of ten thousand proofs. It is taken for granted that free will is preserved and that this qualifies either for praise or blame from us.[20]

3   If, then, our free will is preserved, its future, with its numerous inclinations to virtue or to vice or toward what is fitting or toward what is improper, must, like other things, be known to God from the creation and foundation of the world. And in all that God prearranges in accordance with what he has seen with regard to each act of our free will it has been prearranged that what is fitting to each action under free will be met from his providence and in accordance with the succession of things to come. Yet the foreknowledge of God is not the cause of all things that are to come about, and of all the actions that are to be performed out of our desire and in our free will. For if, for sake of argument, God were ignorant of the future, we would not be thereby absolved from performing some actions and from willing them. Rather, our individual free will receives direction from his foreknowledge so that everything may be usefully arranged with a view to the constitution of the world.

4   If, then, the free will of each individual is known to him, and therefore what is best for each, and most fitting, is foreseen and prearranged in his providence, so indeed he also pre-comprehends how each will pray, and with what disposition, and with what faith, and what his desire is to be. Since this is understood in advance, this has accordingly been arranged somewhat after this manner: To this one, who prays wisely, will I listen when he makes his prayer. To this other will I not listen, either because he is to be undeserving of a hearing

---

[20]There are numerous allusions to sophistic practice in this paragraph. The object of oratory was the ascription of praise or blame, and leading up to this ascription was a series of proofs, stated by way of confirmation or refutation of a proposition.

or else because he will pray for things which it is not profitable for him, a suppliant, to receive, or proper for me to grant. And he says something like: "In the case of this prayer of a particular person I will not listen to him, but in that other I will." And if anyone is disturbed because God, who does not lie, has foreknown the future, since this suggests that matters are predetermined, I must say to him that it is unfailingly known to God that a particular person will not unfailingly and firmly desire the better or will so want the worse that he will be incapable of making any change toward what is profitable.

And again: "These things will I do for this man when he prays, for it is fitting for me, since he will be without reproach in his prayer to me and will not be careless in his approach to prayer. To that man who prays a certain amount I shall grant more than he asks or conceives (Eph 3.20) since it is proper for me to overcome him in kindness and provide more than he can ask. To this other person who will be of a particular character I shall send this angel to assist him, to work with him from a certain time for his salvation and to be with him until a certain time. To that person, one of a higher rank, so to speak, than the other, as he shall be a better person. From that person, who, after devoting himself to more exalted words, will gradually backslide and fall back on more material things, shall I withdraw the superior co-worker so that, at his withdrawal, the inferior power, finding an opportunity to fix upon him in view of his slackness, will be on hand to incite him to certain sins, seeing that he gave himself over into a sinful condition."

5   So we may imagine that the one who orders all things is saying: "Amos will beget Josiah, who will not emulate his father's faults, but will find the way which leads on to virtue, and through those who are with him will be honorable and good, and will overthrow the altar which Jereboam wickedly built (cf. 4 Kg 23.4–25). I also know that Judas, when my son is dwelling among the human race, shall at the beginning be honorable and good, yet later he will turn aside and fall into human sins, on account of which he will rightly suffer in this way."

This foreknowledge, perhaps with regard to all things, but at least concerning Judas and other mysteries, exists also in the Son of God. For, in his understanding of the evolution of things yet to be, he saw Judas and the sins he would commit, and in his comprehension, and before Judas came into existence, said through David: "God, do not be keep silence at my praise," and the rest (Ps 108.1). Seeing what would come to be, and the extent to which Paul would tend to godliness, "Of myself, before the creation of the world or embarking on the fashioning of the world, I will choose him. I will commit him to those powers that work together for human salvation at the moment of his birth, setting him apart from his mother's womb. I shall permit him at first, in his youth, to fall into an ignorant zeal, and on the pretense of godliness to persecute those who have put their faith in my Christ, and to keep the clothes of those who stone my servant and martyr Stephen, so that later, when his willful youth is over and he has turned to the better, he may yet not boast before me but say: 'I am not fit to be called an apostle, because I persecuted the church of God' (1 Cor 15.9). And realizing the future kindness he will receive from me, after the faults of his youth on the pretense of godliness, he may declare: 'I am what I am through the grace of God.' And being restrained by conscience, on account of the acts he performed against Christ whilst young, he will not be puffed up through the abundance of revelations which I shall manifest to him in my kindness" (cf. 2 Cor 12.7).

7

And to the objection with reference to prayer for the rising of the sun, we may reply as follows: The sun also has a certain free will, and since he praises God together with the moon ("Praise him, sun and moon" [Ps 148.3], it says), so it is manifest that the same is true of the moon, and consequently of all the stars as it says: "Praise him all stars and light" (Ps 148.3). So just as we have stated that God employs the free wills of individuals on earth, and disposes them appropriately as is needful for those on earth, likewise we should understand that he employs the free will of the sun and the moon and the stars, fixed and firm, steadfast and wise as it is, and that he arrays the entire world of the heavens, and the course and movement of the stars in harmony with the whole. So if I do not pray in vain with regard to a matter which concerns another's free will, much more is this true when it concerns the free will of the stars of the sky, which contribute to the well-being of the whole as they pursue their course. It may indeed be said of those on the earth that there are certain sense-impressions, received from our environment, which call forth what is weak in us, or else what is for the good, so that we are inclined to speak or act in this way or in that. But what sense-impressions might interpose, and oust or derange heavenly beings from a course that is of benefit to the whole world, since each is in possession of a soul that is fashioned by reason and is entirely self-motivated, and since they employ bodies so ethereal and supremely pure?[21]

8

1   Still, it is not unreasonable to use an example like the following for the encouragement of prayer and to discourage the neglect of prayer. For just as there can be no making of children without a woman and without the desire which accompanies and brings about the making of children, so none might obtain particular things except by praying in this way: with a particular disposition, believing in a certain way, having lived in a certain way prior to prayer. So we are not to babble (Mt 6.7), nor ask after petty things, nor are we to plead for earthly things, nor come to prayer in anger and with our thoughts confused. Without purity it is not possible to consider

[21]Although this may seem a strange argument, the ancient world took it for granted that the heavenly bodies were living beings. For Origen's particular view of the souls of the heavenly bodies, see *On First Principles* 1.7.4. For a discussion of the understanding and status of stars as living beings both in Origen's work and in the ancient world more generally see Alan Scott, *Origen and the life of the stars* (Oxford: Clarendon Press, 1991).

giving oneself over to prayer, nor is it possible to obtain forgiveness of sins in prayer unless one has forgiven from the heart one's brother who has trespassed and has asked to receive pardon.

2   Benefit accrues to the one who prays as one ought to pray, or who seeks to do so according to his ability, in many ways, I think. First, it is a great advantage to fix one's mind upon prayer, through this composure to be present to God, and to speak to him who is present as one who both looks upon us and who hears.[22] For just as certain sense-impressions and memories of such things, which give rise to recollection, may confuse thinking relating to sense-impressions, so we should believe that it is beneficial to have recollection of the God in whom we have put our trust, the one who discerns the movements in the shrine of our souls, as it disposes itself to be pleasing to the One who is present, who looks upon us, who penetrates every mind and who "examines hearts and searches out kidneys" (Ps 7.10). Even though we might suppose that no further benefit comes about for the one who has fixed his mind on prayer, we must realize that the one who so devoutly disposes himself at the time of prayer receives no ordinary result. When this is undertaken frequently, from how many sins does it keep us, to how many righteous deeds does it lead us! This is known from experience by those who have most constantly given themselves to prayer. For if the memory and recollection of a man who is renowned and who has found benefit in wisdom encourages us the more to emulate him and often restrains our impulses to do evil, how much more should the recollection of God who is the father of all, together with prayer to him, give advantage to those who believe that they are present to him, and that they are speaking to a God who is present and who hears them.

9

1   What has been said may be demonstrated from the divine Scriptures in the following manner. The one who prays should lift

[22]The manuscript has "is present" again. This is a conjectural emendation.

up holy hands by forgiving anyone who has done him wrong, banishing the passion of anger from his soul, bearing antagonism to no one. And, so that his mind be not disturbed by extraneous thoughts, at the time of prayer he should forget everything apart from prayer. Is this not a state of supreme blessedness! So Paul teaches in the first letter to Timothy, when he says: "I desire therefore that men should pray in every place, lifting up holy hands free of anger and dissent" (1 Tim 2.8). Beyond this, a woman ought, most of all while at prayer, to maintain simplicity and decency both in soul and body, giving reverence to God while she prays and excluding from her motivation all licentious and womanly thought and adorned not "with a lavish hairstyle and gold, or pearls, or expensive clothes" but adorned as is fitting for a woman who makes a profession of piety. Indeed it amazes me that anyone should hesitate to say that anyone who presents herself for prayer with such a disposition is blessed on the basis of this alone. So Paul taught in the same letter, when he says: "Women likewise, in seemly clothing, should adorn themselves with modesty and discretion, not with a lavish hairstyle and gold, or pearls, or expensive clothes but, in a manner fitting women who profess piety, with good works" (1 Tim 2.9–10).

2   And besides, the prophet David speaks of much else that the saint has in prayer, which may now be set down without irrelevance. Here, for the greatest benefit even if this alone is considered, is made manifest the attitude and the preparation for prayer of one who has committed himself to God. He says: "Up to you, dwelling in heaven, have I lifted my eyes" (Ps 122.1), and "I have lifted up my soul to you, O God" (Ps 24.1). For the eyes are lifted up from interest in earthly matters and from satisfaction with the perception of material things and are so lifted up that they look beyond whatever is begotten and contemplate God alone, and hold modest and solemn converse with the one who hears them. Such people afford the greatest benefit to their eyes, looking upon the glory of the Lord with face unveiled, and so being transformed into his image, from glory to glory (2 Cor 3.18). So they come to share in the outpouring of the divine mind, as

is made clear in the phrase: "Lord, the light of your face has been signed upon us" (Ps 4.7). And the soul which is lifted up and which, separated from the body, follows the Spirit, which not only follows the Spirit but is actually in the Spirit (as is made clear in the phrase: "I have lifted up my soul to you") is surely putting off its existence as a soul and becoming spiritual.[23]

3   And if forgetfulness of wrongdoing is such a mighty accomplishment that, according to the prophet Jeremiah it is a summary of the whole law, when he says: "I did not lay these commands on your fathers when they came out of Egypt, but this command I did lay down: 'Let nobody recall a neighbor's sins in his heart,'"[24] and when we come to prayer without being mindful of wrongdoing we keep the commandment of the Savior: "If you are standing at prayer, forgive whatever you have against anybody" (Mk 11.25), then it is plain that those who stand to pray in this state have already received the best there is.

10

1   We have said all this on the basis that, if nothing else should accrue to us in praying, we have nonetheless received the best of gains by praying with understanding of the manner in which we should pray and keeping to this. For it is obvious that anyone who prays in this manner, concentrating on the power of the one who listens and having cast away all discontent with providence, will, while he is still speaking, hear "Here I am." This is indicated by the phrase: "If you have put off the bonds from yourself, and pointing the finger and murmuring" (Is 58.9). For whoever is best pleased with whatever should occur is made free from every bond, and does not put out a hand against God who ordains whatever he wishes for our training and does not even murmur secretly in his thoughts with a

---

[23]Cf. the treatment of the soul being joined to the spirit leading a person to be spiritual in *On First Principles* 3.4.2.

[24]Actually a conflation of Jer 7.22–23 and Zech 7.10.

voice which cannot be humanly heard. Such is the manner in which bad domestic servants murmur, not openly opposing their masters' instructions. In this manner do they murmur, not daring to speak ill of providence out loud or wholeheartedly for whatever has happened, but as though they wished to hide the extent of their displeasure from the Lord of all things. And I think that this is what is meant by the passage in Job: "And in all that happened Job did no wrongdoing with his lips before the Lord" (Job 2.10), whilst it is written regarding the previous testing: "In all that happened Job did no wrongdoing in the sight of the Lord." And the statement which, in Deuteronomy, makes provision for what should not occur is: "Take heed that there be in your heart no hidden thought of lawbreaking, saying 'The seventh year is approaching' " (Deut 15.9) and so on.

2   Therefore whoever prays in this manner, and is so greatly enriched, becomes yet more ready to be mingled with the Spirit of the Lord who fills the whole world (Wis 1.7) and fills all the earth and the heaven, who speaks thus through the prophet: " 'Do I not fill the heaven and the earth,' says the Lord" (Jer 23.24). Furthermore, through the purity of which we have spoken as through prayer, he shall come to share in the Word of God who stands in the midst even of those who do not know him, who disregards the prayer of nobody, and who prays to the Father together with the one on whose behalf he mediates. For the Son of God is high priest of our offerings and advocate with the Father (1 Jn 2.1). He prays on behalf of those who pray and acts as advocate together with those who plead, though he will not pray as for his friends if they will not pray habitually through him, nor will he be an advocate to God as for his own people unless they are obedient to his teaching that they should pray at all times and not lose heart. As it says: "He spoke a parable to the effect that they ought to pray at all times and not lose heart. A certain judge there was in a certain city . . ." and so on (Lk 18.1–2). And prior to this: "And he said to them: 'Which of you would have a friend, and would go to him in the middle of the night and say to him: "Friend, lend me three loaves, since a friend of mine on a

journey has come to me and I have nothing to set before him" ' "
(Lk 11.5–6). And a little later: "I tell you, even if he does not get up
and give them to him for the sake of friendship, yet he will get up
and give him as many as he needs because of his shamelessness"
(Lk 11.8). And of those who trust in the guileless mouth of Jesus, who
shall not be stirred to unhesitating prayer when he says: "Ask, and it
will be given you. For whoever asks, receives" (Lk 11.9–10). For the
good Father gives living bread to those who ask him, to those who
have received the Spirit of adoption (Rom 8.15) from the Father, and
not the stone that the adversary wants made into bread for Jesus and
his disciples. And the Father gives the good gift, raining it from
heaven upon those who ask him (Lk 11.13; cf. Ex 16.4).

11

1   Not only does the high priest pray alongside those who pray
authentically, but those who are in heaven, the angels who "rejoice
over one sinner who repents more than over ninety-nine just persons who have no need of repentance" (Lk 15.7), and likewise the
souls of the saints who have gone to their rest.[25] This is demonstrated when Raphael offers rational worship to God on behalf of
Tobit and Sara. For after they had prayed, the prayer of them both,
says the Scripture, was heard. "The prayer of them both (was heard)
before the majesty of the mighty Raphael and he was sent to heal
them both" (Tobit 3.16–17). And Raphael himself, revealing God's
plan to them both, as an angel subject to the commandment of God,
says: "Now, when you and your daughter-in-law Sara prayed, I
brought the remembrance of your request before the Holy One"
(Tobit 12.12). And a little later: "I am Raphael, one of the seven angels
which present the prayers of the saints and who enter before the

---

[25]Although the case for angelic and sanctoral assistance is supported by scriptural arguments, this fits closely with Platonic ideas of intermediate classes of beings
between God and creation, which served to put distance between the unchangeable
God and the changing terrestrial order.

glory of the Lord."²⁶ Thus, according to the account of Raphael, "prayer with fasting and almsgiving and righteousness is good" (Tobit 12.8). Moreover Jeremiah appears in the books of the Maccabees so resplendent in "white-haired glory" that "the excellency which surrounded him was wonderful and majestic" and he stretched forth his "right hand and handed Judas a sword of gold." To whom another saint who has gone to rest bore witness, saying: "This is the one who intercedes often for the people and for the holy city, Jeremiah the prophet of God" (2 Macc 15.13–15).

2   And when knowledge is revealed in the present to those who are worthy "through a glass" and "as a puzzle," later to be revealed "face to face" (1 Cor 13.12), it is absurd to suppose that the same is not true of the other virtues, for it is certain that those things for which we are prepared in this life will be made perfect.

Now the highest of virtues, according to the divine word, is love toward one's neighbor; surely we must impute this to the saints who have gone to their rest before us toward those who are struggling in this life, more so than those who, in human weakness, struggle alongside those who are yet weaker. For it is not only here below that "if one limb should suffer, all the limbs suffer with it." "And if one limb is glorified, all the limbs rejoice with it" (1 Cor 12.26) applies to those who love their brothers. For it is fitting that those who are outside this present life should say, in love, ". . . the care of all the churches. Who is there who is weak, and I am not weak also? Who is there who is offended, and I am not inflamed?" (2 Cor 11.28–29) Especially since Christ confesses that whenever one of the saints is in weakness he is likewise in weakness, and that he is likewise in prison, and is imprisoned, and is naked, a stranger, and that he hungers and thirsts (Mt 25.35–36). For who, of those acquainted with the Gospel, does not know that Christ, by taking on himself whatever should befall believers, reckons these to be his own sufferings?

---

²⁶Tobit 12.15. This is cited here in accordance with the Septuagint. The manuscript does not have the words concerning the prayers of the saints in this citation.

3   And if angels of God came to Jesus and served him (Mt 4.11), and if it is not fitting that we should consider that the angels' service to Jesus is for a short period, while he was bodily dwelling amongst people, and while he was in the midst of those who believe, not as one who sits down to eat but who serves, how many angels, I wonder, are likely to serve Jesus when he desires to "bring together the children of Israel one by one" (Is 27.12; Jn 11.52) and to gather in the dispersion, saving those who fear him and call upon him (Acts 2.21; Rom 10.13), working with him even more than the apostles in the increase and expansion of the church. Thus angels are said to be set over some of the churches by John in the Apocalypse. For the angels of God do not go up and come down "upon the son of man" (Jn 1.51) without reason, as they are seen by eyes which are enlightened by the light of knowledge.

4   And therefore, on the occasion of prayer, they are reminded of the things he needs by the person who prays and, insofar as they are able, they bring it about, since they have received a comprehensive instruction so to do.

We may use an illustration of this doctrine in order to make our meaning clear. Suppose that a doctor, of righteous mind, is standing by one who is sick and is praying for health. He is knowledgeable of the manner in which the disease about which the man is offering prayer is to be treated. It is manifest that he would be moved to heal the one who prays, perhaps, and not without reason, understanding that this was in the mind of God, who heard the prayer of the person who prayed for release from the disease. Or suppose that one who is more than wealthy in the necessities of life should hear the prayer of a poor person who lifts up an appeal to God on account of his necessity. It is obvious that he will fulfill the prayer of the poor person, becoming a minister of the will of the Father who, on the occasion of prayer, brought the one who was able to share and who, because of the rightness of his character, was unable to overlook the person in need, together with the one who prayed.

5   Just as we are not to think that these things, when they happen, occur by chance, since the one who has numbered all the hairs on the head of the saints (Mt 10.30) aptly brings together, on the occasion of prayer, the one who hears, who is to be a minister of kindness to the one in need, and the person who has prayed in faith, so we should understand that sometimes the presence of the angels, who exercise oversight and service for God, is brought together for somebody who is praying, so that they can join in giving breath to the requests which he is making. But more than this, the angel of each of us, even of "little ones" in the church, who for ever look upon the face of the Father in heaven (Mt 18.10) and on the divinity of the one who formed us, prays alongside us and acts together with us, as much as is possible, with regard to the matters concerning which we pray.

12

1   I believe that the words of the prayer of the saints are full of power, especially when, in their prayer, they are praying "in the Spirit and with the understanding" (1 Cor 14.15), by the light, so to speak, which arises from the mind of the one who prays and goes forth from his mouth to dissolve, by the power of God, the spiritual poison which is injected by the enemy powers into the mind of any who neglect prayer and who do not observe the words of Paul, following the exhortations given by Jesus, that we should "pray ceaselessly" (1 Thess 5.17). For like a dart from the soul of the one who prays with knowledge and with reason or by faith will it go forth from the saint, and wound to destruction and dissolution the spirits which are hostile to God, those who desire to truss us with the bonds of sin.

2   Since works of virtue and the keeping of the commandments have a part in prayer, the person who prays "ceaselessly" is the one who integrates prayer with good works and noble actions with prayer. For we can only accept the saying "Pray ceaselessly" as realistic if we say that the whole life of the saint is one mighty, integrated

prayer.[27] Of this prayer, part is what is usually termed "prayer," and this should not be performed less than three times each day. This is evident from the account of Daniel, who, when great danger threatened, prayed three times daily (Dan 6.10). Likewise Peter, who went up to the housetop to pray at around the sixth hour, when he saw the vessel let down from heaven, let down by its four corners (Acts 10.9–11), exemplifies the middle of the three hours, of which David previously had spoken:[28] "In the morning you shall hear my prayer: in the morning shall I present myself to you and I shall look upon you" (Ps 5.4). And the last is indicated in the words: "The raising of my hands as an evening sacrifice." Indeed, we should acknowledge that the night is not without a fitting occasion of prayer for, as David says: "In the middle of the night I got up to give you thanks because of your righteous judgments" (Ps 118.62). Paul, as the Acts of the Apostles tells us, was praying and singing hymns to God together with Silas at Philippi at around midnight, so that the prisoners also heard them (Acts 16.25).

13

1   If Jesus prays and does not pray in vain, since he obtains what he asks through prayer, and since he might not have received this except through praying, which of us can neglect prayer? For Mark says that "early in the morning, well before dawn, he arose and went to a deserted place, and he prayed there" (Mk 1.35). And Luke: "It so happened when he was in a particular place praying, when he

[27]Cf. Clement's treatment of this saying at *Stromata* 7.7.

[28]Note that the citation does not fit with Peter's prayer at midday. E. G. Jay (*Origen's Treatise on Prayer* [London: SPCK, 1954], 115) solves the difficulty by suggesting that night is the first occasion of prayer, and that prayer at midday might be counted as morning prayer! Night, however, is not one of the three occasions of the day, but is additional. The difficulty remains, but we may observe that Origen provides a scriptural exemplar for each of the three times of prayer in the course of the day and for that in the night. For further discussion of these times of prayer, see the appendix to the introduction.

ceased, one of his disciples said to him . . ." (Lk 11.1) and elsewhere: "And he spent the entire night in prayer to God" (Lk 6.12). John records his prayer, saying: "Jesus said these things, and lifting up his eyes to heaven he said: 'Father, the hour has come. Glorify your son so that your son might glorify you' " (Jn 17.1). And the Lord's saying, "I knew that you always hear me" (Jn 11.42), recorded by the same [evangelist], shows that whoever always prays is always heard.

2   What need is there to make a list of those who, through praying in the manner in which we should, have obtained the greatest blessings from God, since each may choose for himself a great many from the Scriptures? Hannah did service in the birth of Samuel, who is to be reckoned alongside Moses (Jer 15.1), because when she was childless she prayed in faith to the Lord (1 Kg 1.10). Hezekiah, whilst he was yet without issue, prayed to the Lord when he learnt from Isaiah that he was about to die, and was admitted into the genealogy of the Savior. And when, because of a single decree deriving from Haman's plot, the entire people was about to be destroyed, the prayer with fasting of Mordecai and Esther was heard, so that, in addition to the feasts according to Moses, there came about the day of Mordecai, when the people rejoice (Esth 3.6; 4.16; 9.26). But Judith too, having offered holy prayer, overcomes Holofernes with the help of God, and so a single Hebrew woman brought shame on the house of Nebuchadnezzar (Jdt 13.4–9). And Ananias, Azarias, and Mizael were heard, and were considered fit to receive a "whispering wind of dew" which did not allow the flame of the fire to take effect (Dan 3.50). In the Babylonian den the lions were muzzled through Daniel's prayers (Dan 6.22), and even Jonah, because he did not despair of being heard from the belly of the monster which had swallowed him, emerges from the belly of the monster so that he could fulfill what was wanting of prophecy toward the Ninevites (Jon 3.1).

3   Should any of us recall with gratitude how many kindnesses we have received, how much could we each recount, and so wish to offer up praises to God! For souls that had long been barren have realized the sterility of their own motivation and the barrenness of their own

minds, and have become pregnant from the Holy Spirit through constancy in prayer, and have given birth to words of salvation filled with the perception of truth. How many of our foes, when so often thousands of malignant powers have encamped against us and sought to cut us off from divine faith, have been dispersed. Some trust "in chariots" and some "in horses" but we by calling on "the name of the Lord" (Ps 19.8), and so we are encouraged, when we see that indeed "a horse is a vain thing for safety" (Ps 32.17). Indeed, the person who has believed can, through praise to God, cut down even the captain of the adversary, guileful and persuasive speech, which causes many, even of those considered to have faith, to tremble. For "Judith" is to be interpreted as "praise." What need is there to speak of those many who have so often fallen among trials which burn more fiercely than any flame, which are so hard to overcome, and have suffered from them not at all, but emerged in every way unharmed, unscathed by even a sniff of the enemy's fire? Or how many wild beasts ranged against us in the form of evil spirits or cruel people have we encountered, muzzling them so often through prayer, so that they could not fasten their teeth onto our limbs, which have become those of Christ? For frequently, for each of the saints, has the Lord "broken the teeth of the lions, and brought them to nothing, like water flowing by" (Ps 57.7–8). We know that often those who have fled from the commandments of God, swallowed up by the death that previously overpowered them, have, through repentance, been rescued from such evil, because they did not despair of the possibility of salvation, even when they were held fast in the belly of death. "For death overpowered them and swallowed them up, but God, again, wiped away every tear from every face" (Is 25.8).

4   I reckon that it was most necessary that I should say these things, after enumerating the benefits received through prayer, as a means of turning those aspiring to the spiritual life in Christ away from prayer for petty and earthly concerns and summoning those who read this writing toward mystical matters, of which the

matters above mentioned were types. For every prayer for the spiritual and mystical gifts that we have instanced is brought to completion by the one who does not war in accordance with the flesh (2 Cor 10.3) but who, through the Spirit, does to death the deeds of the body (Rom 8.13). For we should give preference to whatever, after study, is presented by analogy, over the obvious blessings that, according to the surface meaning, were supplied to those who prayed. We are to train ourselves so that barrenness and sterility should not come about as we listen to the spiritual law with spiritual ears; then, when we lay aside our barren and sterile state, we may be heard as were Hannah and Hezekiah, and, like Mordecai, and Esther, and Judith, be delivered from spiritual foes who wish to do us harm. And just as Egypt is an iron furnace (Deut 4.20; Jer 11.4), and a symbol of every earthly place, everybody who has escaped the evil of human life and is unscorched by sin, whose heart is not full of fire like a baking pot,[29] should give thanks no less than they who experienced the dew in the fire. And whoever has prayed and said: "Do not deliver to the wild beasts the soul which has confessed you" (Ps 73.19) (and has been heard, and has suffered nothing from the asp or the basilisk because, through Christ, he has trodden on them and has "trampled the lion and the dragon" [Ps 90.13], and has made use of the glorious authority given by Christ to "walk over serpents and scorpions and upon the whole power of the enemy" [Lk 10.19] and been untouched by them), should give thanks even more than Daniel, since he has been delivered from wild beasts yet more fearsome and more harmful. Anyone, moreover, who is aware of the nature of the monster typified by that which swallowed Jonah, who perceives that this is described by Job when he says: "Let him curse it, who curses that day, who is ready to take on the great monster" (Job 3.8), should pray in repentance should he ever find himself "in the belly of the monster"

---

[29]A baking pot was something like a casserole dish which, being surrounded by hot embers, distributed heat evenly. It was thus less "full of fire" than full of heat. See however, 30.3 below, with its citation of Hos 7.6, which may illuminate Origen's use of the word here.

through some act of disobedience, and he will emerge from it. And if, when he comes out, he remains obedient to the commandments of God, he shall be able, through the goodness of the Spirit, to prophesy to the Ninevites who are at present being destroyed and to be the means of their salvation, neither being discontented with the goodness of God, nor desiring that he should continue in severity toward those who repent.[30]

5   Everyone who is genuinely dependent upon God, and has become worthy of being heard, can now, in a spiritual sense, perform the mightiest act, which Samuel is said to have performed through prayer. For it is written: "Now, then, stand and see this great deed which the Lord performs before your eyes. Is it not the harvest of wheat today? I shall call upon the Lord and he shall send thunder and rain." Then, a little later, it says: "And Samuel called upon the Lord, and the Lord sent thunder and rain on that day" (1 Kg 12.16–18). For to all who are holy and to all who are genuine disciples of Jesus, the Lord says: "Lift up your eyes and look at the fields; they are white already for the harvest. Whoever reaps gathers a reward and garners fruit for eternal life" (Jn 4.35–36). In this harvest season the Lord performs a great deed before the eyes of those who listen to the prophets. For when anyone who is accompanied by the Holy Spirit calls upon the Lord, God sends thunder from heaven and rain to irrigate the soul. Whoever previously was living in vice may come to fear the Lord greatly, as well as may the minister of the grace of God, since, through the hearing of his prayer, he is shown to be worthy of reverence and honor. When the heavens were closed to the impious for three years and six months, Elijah opened them with a divine word.[31] This may be achieved at any time by anyone who, having been drought-stricken through sin, through prayer receives rain for the soul.

---

[30]This reading incorporates a conjecture of Anglus.
[31]3 Kg 17; 18; cf. Jas 5.17–18.

14

1   Now that we have given an interpretation of the blessings which have come about for the saints through prayer, let us turn our attention to the saying: "Ask for the great things and the petty things shall be added to you. And ask for heavenly things and mundane things shall be added to you."[32] Now all those things that are symbols and types are petty and earthly in comparison to those that are true and spiritual. It seems probable that the divine Word, in exhorting us to imitate the prayers of the saints, is pointing to the heavenly and great things which are expressed in the earthly and the petty, so that we might make our requests according to the reality of which the achievements of the saints was a type. In effect it says: "You that desire to be spiritual, so request great and heavenly things,[33] so that when you attain them you shall become inheritors of the Kingdom of heaven and so enjoy the best of good things, as your Father will supply, in accordance with your need, the earthly and petty things which you use for the body out of necessity."

2   Now since, in the first Epistle to Timothy, the apostle speaks of four topics related to the subject of prayer by using four terms, it would be useful to examine what he says, to cite the words and to see, by careful examination, if we have properly understood the meaning of each of the four terms. This is what he says: "First, I exhort you to make supplication, intercession, pleas and thanksgiving for everyone" (1 Tim 2.1) and so on.[34] Now, I think that "supplication" is the prayer that is offered with pleading, by somebody who is lacking something, so that it might be obtained. That prayer is offered up by somebody more high-minded and is accompanied by ascription of glory. That an appeal is an address requesting something that is made to God with boldness. That thanksgiving is a

---

[32]The first part of the phrase is Mt 6.33. The second part, also cited by Origen at 2.2 above, may be an Alexandrian variant in the text.

[33]The words "great and heavenly things" after "request" are not in the manuscript, and are inserted following a suggestion of Anglus.

[34]The four terms are: *deēsis*, *proseuchē*, *enteuxis*, and *eucharistia*.

response made by somebody who, after prayer, has received good things from God; the response is an acknowledgement of the greatness of the blessing, as the greatness of the blessing appears to the one on whom it is bestowed.

3   As examples of the first we may take that which Gabriel said toward Zechariah, who surely had prayed regarding the birth of John. "Do not be afraid, Zechariah," he said, "since your supplication has been heard, and your wife Elizabeth shall bear you a son, and you shall name him John" (Lk 1.13). And, in Exodus, it is written thus concerning the making of the calf: "And Moses made supplication before the Lord God and said: 'Why are you heated with anger, Lord, against your people, which you led out of Egypt with great might?'" (Ex 32.11) And in Deuteronomy: "And I made supplication before the Lord a second time, just as I did before, for forty days and forty nights, regarding all the sins which you committed. And I ate no bread and drank no water" (Deut 9.18). And in the book of Esther: "Mordecai made supplication of God, and remembered all the words of the Lord, and said: 'Lord, Lord, almighty King" (Esth 13.8–9). And Esther herself "made supplication to the Lord, the God of Israel, and said: 'Lord our king . . .'"

4   There is an example of the second in Daniel: "And Azarias drew himself up and, opening his mouth, interceded in the middle of the fire, saying . . ." (Dan 3.25). And in Tobit: "And he interceded with sorrow, saying: 'Lord, you are just, as are all your works, all your works are mercy and truth, and your judgment is true and you judge righteously for ever" (Tobit 3.1–2). However, since those of the circumcision mark the passage in Daniel with an obelus, as it is not extant in the Hebrew,[35] and since they reject the book of Tobit as not being in the Testament, I may add the case of Hannah in the first book of Kingdoms: "And she interceded with the Lord and wept

[35]This passage as a whole would be recognized in the ancient world as belonging to the realm of the grammarian. The correction of texts and observations of textual variants was part of this realm, and so this observation on the text of Tobit belongs entirely in its context.

despondently. And she vowed a vow and said: 'Lord of hosts, if indeed you will look upon your servant's affliction' " and the rest (1 Kg 1.10–11). And in Habakkuk: "Intercession of Habakkuk the prophet, with a canticle: Lord, I have listened to your voice and I was awe-struck. Lord, I have considered your works and was astonished. In the midst of two living beings shall you be known; you shall be recognized in the approach of the years" (Hab 3.1–2). This is an excellent illustration of what I said in defining prayer, that prayer is offered up with an ascription of glory. But also in Jonah: "Jonah interceded with the Lord his God from the belly of the monster and said: 'I called out to the Lord my God in my affliction, and he listened to me. From the belly of hell you listened to the sound of my crying. You flung me into the depths of the heart of the sea, and the streams surrounded me' " (Jon 2.2–4).

5   There is an example of the third in the apostle, where he rightly attributes intercession to ourselves, but pleading to the Spirit, which excels ourselves and has boldness in approaching the one with whom he pleads. For, he says, "We do not know the manner in which we should pray, or for what, but the Spirit itself, with unutterable groanings, pleads with God. And the one who searches out hearts knows what the mind of the Spirit is, because his pleading with God on behalf of the saints is in accordance with God's will" (Rom 8.26–27). For the Spirit pleads, and does more than plead, whereas we "intercede."

That which is said by Joshua concerning the standing still of the sun over Gibeon seems to me to be a plea. "So spoke Joshua to the Lord, on the day on which God delivered the Amorites into the hand of Israel, when he crushed them in Gibeon and they were crushed from the face of the children of Israel. And Joshua said: 'Let the sun stand over Gibeon, and the moon over the valley of Elom' " (Josh 10.12). And I think that Samson, in the book of Judges, was making a plea when he said: "Let my soul perish with the aliens." Then "he leant mightily and the house fell on the princes and on all the people who were in it" (Judg 16.30). Although it does not state that they were making a plea, but that Joshua and Samson "said," the nature of their speech seems to be that of pleading. And should we give strict definition to the terms, this seems to be distinct from "intercession."

An example of thanksgiving is that to which the Lord gave utterance when he says: "I make confession to you, Father, Lord of heaven and earth, because you have hidden these things from the wise, and those of understanding, and have revealed them to the simple" (Lk 10.21). For "I make confession" is equivalent to "I give thanks."

6   Now supplication and plea and thanksgiving may be offered to people without impropriety. Two of them, namely pleading and thanksgiving, might be offered not only to saints but to people in general, whereas supplication should be offered to saints alone,[36] should there be found a Paul or a Peter, who may benefit us and make us worthy to attain authority for the forgiveness of sins. If, indeed, we do wrong to somebody who is not a saint, when we perceive the extent to which we have sinned against him we may supplicate a person like this that he might extend pardon to us who have done him wrong. Yet if these things are to be offered to saints, how much more should we give thanks to Christ, who extends such blessings to us in accordance with the Father's will! But we are also to plead with him, as did Stephen when he said: "Lord, do not set this sin against them" (Acts 7.60). And should we say, "I beg you, Lord, have mercy on my son" (Lk 9.38) or "on me" or on anyone at all, we shall be imitating the father of the lunatic.

15

1   Now if we observe the proper nature of prayer we should not pray to any begotten being, not even to Christ himself, but only to

---

[36]The passage is translated as found in the manuscript. However, the text is often emended to read as follows: "Now supplication and plea and thanksgiving may be offered to people who are saints without impropriety. Two of them, namely pleading and thanksgiving, might be offered not only to saints but to other people, whereas supplication should be offered to saints alone."

God the Father of all, to whom even our Savior himself prayed, as we have already recorded, and to whom he teaches us to pray. For when he heard: "Teach us to pray" (Lk 11.1), he does not teach us to pray to himself but to the Father. "Our Father, who are in the heavens . . ." and the rest. For if, as is shown elsewhere, the Son is distinct from the Father in essence and in underlying reality,[37] then we should pray to the Son and not to the Father, or to them both, or to the Father alone. That prayer to the Son and not to the Father is absurd, and contrary to obvious evidence, would be universally agreed. Whereas if we are to pray to both it is clear that we should have to offer our requests in plural form, saying as we pray: "Grant, both of you," and "Bless, both of you," "Supply, both of you," "Save, both of you," and the like. This is self-evidently incongruous, and nor can anybody show that this is to be found spoken by anyone in the Scriptures. It therefore remains to us to pray to God the Father of all alone, but not apart from the high priest, who has been appointed by the Father by the swearing of an "oath that he will not revoke. You are a priest for ever, after the order of Melchizedek" (Ps 109.4).

2   Therefore the saints, when they give thanks to God in their prayers, confess their thanks to him through Jesus Christ. Just as it is improper for somebody who is scrupulous in prayer to pray to one who himself prays but to the one whom our Lord Jesus taught us to address as "Father" in our prayers, so no prayer should be offered to the Father except through him;[38] as he himself made clear when he said: "Truly, truly I say to you, if you should ask anything of my Father, he will grant it you in my name. Until now you have asked nothing in my name; ask, and you shall receive, so that your joy may be completed" (Jn 16.23–24). For he did not say: "Ask me," or simply

---

[37]"*kat' ousian kai hupokeimenon*." This is not the place for a discussion of the possible significance of this passage for Origen's overall theology. For such a discussion see W. Gessel, *Die Theologie des Gebetes nach "De Oratione" von Origenes* (Munich: Schöningh, 1975), 96–101.

[38]Cf. *Dialogue with Heraclides* 1.1–6.5.

"Ask the Father," but "If you should ask anything of the Father he will grant it you in my name." For until Jesus taught this, nobody besought the Father in the name of the Son, so Jesus' words, "until now you have asked nothing in my name" are true. And true also is the statement: "Ask, and you shall receive, so that your joy may be completed" (Jn 16.24).

3   And if anyone, thinking that we should pray to Christ himself on the basis of what is said of worshipping, and introducing the passage: "Let all the angels of God worship him" (Deut 32.43), which is admittedly said of Christ in Deuteronomy, we should say to him that the Church, which is named Jerusalem by the prophet, is said to be worshipped by kings and queens, who become providers and nurses for her, in this passage: "Behold, I lift up my hand to the gentiles, and to the islands I set up my standard. And they shall bring your sons in their bosom, and your daughters shall they lift on their shoulders. And kings shall be your providers, and queens your nurses. They shall worship you on the face of the earth, and the dust of your feet they shall lick up. And you shall know that I am the Lord, and you will not be put to shame" (Is 49.22–23).

4   And is this not in keeping with his words: "Why do you call me good? Nobody is good except God the Father"? (Mk 10.18) Might he not have said: "Why do you pray to me? You should pray to the Father alone, to whom I likewise pray. Learn this from the Holy Scriptures: for you should not pray to a high priest established by the Father on your behalf, and who has received the office of advocate from the Father, but through a high priest and advocate, who is able to sympathize with your weakness, who was tested in all things just as you but, through the free gift of the Father, was tested and found without sin (Heb 4.15). Learn therefore, what a great gift you have received from my Father through your regeneration in me, through receiving the Spirit of adoption, so that you might be counted sons of God and brothers to me (Rom 8.14–15). For you have read what was said by me to the Father concerning you, through the voice of David: 'I will declare your name to my brothers; in the midst of the

assembly will I sing your praise' (Ps 21.23). It is unreasonable for you to pray to a brother when you have been made worthy of sharing one Father with him. You should offer up your prayer to the Father alone, with me and through me."

16

1   So, when we hear Jesus declare these things, let us pray to God through him, all speaking with one accord and being not divided in the manner of our prayer. Are we not indeed divided if some pray to the Father and others to the Son, those who pray to the Son, whether together with the Father or altogether without the Father, so committing an individual sin in their great simplicity through their lack of discernment and discrimination? Let us pray, therefore, as to God, let us plead as with a Father, let us make supplication as of a Lord, let us give thanks as to God, and to a father, and to a Lord, though a Lord who is not the Lord of a slave. For the Father is rightly counted as Lord, not only of the Son but Lord of all who have, through him, obtained sonship. And as he is "God, not of the dead but of the living" (Mt 22.32), so he is Lord, not of slaves of no birth, but of those who are ennobled, though first in fear because of their immaturity, but who afterward give service out of love, a service which is more blessed than that which is out of fear. For these are the marks of the soul, visible only to the one who looks on the heart, of those who are slaves and sons of God.

2   Anyone, moreover, who asks after mundane and minor matters from God is disregarding the one who commands us to request what is heavenly and great from the God who does not know how to bestow anything mundane or minor. And if anyone should object with regard to the material gifts accorded to the saints through prayer, and the statement in the Gospel which teaches that the mundane and the minor will be added to us, we may reply that, just as when somebody gives us something material we do not say that the person has given us the shadow of the object, for he does not by

intent bestow on us two things, the object and the shadow, but rather that the intention of the giver is to give a material object, and thus that our receipt of the shadow is dependent upon the gift of the object, so, if our mind has become more noble, we might discern the principal gifts which are given us by God, we might say that material things are suitable accompaniments to the great and heavenly spiritual graces which are given to each of the saints for their good (1 Cor 12.7), or in proportion to faith (Rom 12.6), or in accordance with the will of the giver. And his will is wise, even if we are unable to give an account of the cause or a reason worthy of the giver for each of the gifts.

3   Thus the soul of Hannah, when changed from barrenness, bore more fruit than did her body when she conceived Samuel. And Hezekiah begot children more divine from his mind than from his body, when he had children from his bodily seed. And Esther and Mordecai and all the people were delivered from spiritual plots much more than that from Haman and his fellow conspirators. And Judith cut off the might of the ruler who sought to destroy her soul yet more than that of Holophernes.[39] And who would not admit that the spiritual blessing which comes down on all the saints, and of which Isaac spoke to Jacob in saying, "may God give you of the dew of heaven" (Gen 27.28), and which was accorded to Ananias and his companions, was greater than the material dew which vanquished the flame of Nebuchadnezzar? (Dan 3.50) And that the prophet Daniel muzzled unseen lions, who were unable to work any ill against his soul, rather than perceptible ones, to which all who read the Scripture understand that it refers. And who has not escaped from the belly of the monster which swallows every fugitive from God, and which is overcome by Jesus our Savior, as did Jonah, and so, as a saint, became fit to receive the Holy Spirit?

[39]The first part of this sentence is missing in the manuscript. The mention of Judith is therefore conjectural.

17

1   If, so to speak, all objects that are capable of casting a shadow do not cast a shadow that corresponds directly to themselves, whereas others cast a corresponding shadow, it is not to cause surprise. Those who study issues relating to sundials and the relation of shadows to the illuminating body clearly observe this of objects: that at some times the indices are shadowless, at other times the shadow cast is, so to speak, foreshortened, and at others it is extended. And so, as the intention of the giver is to grant the principal gifts in accordance with some unutterable and hidden proportions in keeping with the recipient and the occasion, so it is no great surprise should, when the principal gifts are given, some be altogether unaccompanied by shadows for those who receive, whereas at other times the shadows are but few, and at other times they are reduced in comparison, while others are accompanied by larger shadows. So just as the person who seeks the sun's rays is neither pleased nor pained by the presence or absence of the shadows of objects, in that he has what he most requires, since he has the light shining upon him, whether he is casting a large shadow or a small one, so if we are in possession of spiritual things, and are illuminated by God and are altogether in possession of what is truly good, then we shall not quibble over such a trifling matter as the shadow.[40] For material and physical things, whatsoever they might be, are to be accounted as fleeting and feeble shadows, and are utterly incapable of comparison with the saving acts and holy gifts of the God of all things. For what comparison is there between physical wealth and wealth in every utterance and all wisdom? (1 Cor 1.5) And who but a maniac would compare health of flesh and bones with the health of the spirit and the strength of the soul and with the power of reasoning in accordance with these? All these things, when duly ordered by the Word of God, make any bodily suffering a trifling scratch, or whatever we might consider less than a scratch.

---

[40]Lying behind Origen's thought here are Plato's twin parables of the sun, and of the shadows cast in the cave, at *Republic* 6.508c–509d and 7.514a–517a.

2   Whoever has discerned the meaning of the beauty of the bride whom the bridegroom, which is the Word of God, loves, a soul which blossoms with beauty beyond heaven and earth, will be ashamed to dignify the bodily beauty of a wife or a child or a husband with the name of beauty. For the flesh is not capable of true beauty, for it is thoroughly deformed. For "all flesh is grass" as is its beauty. This is readily observable in the so-called beauty of women and children, as it is compared in the prophetic parable to a flower, in the saying: "All flesh is as grass, and all its glory as the flower of grass. The grass withers, and the flower fades, yet the Word of the Lord remains for ever" (Is 40.6–8). Again, who that has perceived the nobility of the sons of God should still give the name of nobility to what is so commonly called in human circles? And if the mind has contemplated the Kingship of Christ that has sway over kings,[41] it will consider no earthly Kingdom as worthy of the name. And when, insofar as it is able whilst still tied to a body, it clearly sees the army of angels, and the archangels among them as the chief commanders of the Lord's powers, and thrones and dominations and principalities and supercelestial powers (cf. Col 1.16), realizes that it might obtain equal honor with them through the Father's gift, how will it not come to despise those things which, though frailer than a shadow,[42] are the admiration of the foolish, considering them as shadowy and insignificant by comparison, even though they all might be given to it. Will it not overlook them, so as not to fall short of the true principalities and the divine powers? We should pray then, praying for principal gifts, for those that are truly great and heavenly, and the matter of the shadows that accompany these principal gifts should be left to God, who knows what we need for our perishable body "before we ask him" (Mt 6.8).

[41]The text is here emended following Anglus, whose proposed emendation makes the least alteration to the impossible reading of the manuscripts. Others have been proposed.

[42]Again, an emendation of Anglus is accepted. The alternative reading would make the epithet of "feebler than a shadow" refer to the mind, which seems to miss the point.

18

1   In accordance with the grace which has been given by God and through his Christ (and also, I trust, in the Holy Spirit) and insofar as we have received it,[43] we have given sufficient attention to the question of prayer in what has already been said. Whether it be so, you shall judge as you read the treatise. And so we shall pass on to our next task; our intention is to study the prayer outlined by the Lord, full, as it is, of meaning.

2   And it is first of all to be observed that Matthew and Luke appear to most people to have recorded the same prayer as an outline of the manner in which we ought to pray.

Matthew's version reads as follows: "Our Father who are in the heavens, let your name be hallowed, let your Kingdom come, let your will be done—as in heaven so also on earth. Give us today our supersubstantial bread. And forgive us our debts, as we also have forgiven our debtors. And do not bring us into testing, but rescue us from evil."

That of Luke is like this: "Father, let your name be hallowed, let your Kingdom come. Give us our supersubstantial bread daily. And forgive us our sins, as we ourselves pardon everyone indebted to us. And do not bring us into testing."

3   To those who make this supposition we should say first that the wordings, although they have much in common with each other, also appear elsewhere to differ, as we shall demonstrate when we examine them. Second that it is not possible that the same prayer should be said on the mountain as "when Jesus saw the crowds he went up the mountain, and when he sat down his disciples came to him and he opened his mouth and taught them" (Mt 5.1–2), for it is in the passage which concerns the beatitudes and the commands

---

[43]Or, "In accordance with the grace which has been given insofar as we have received it from God and through his Christ (and also, I trust, in the Holy Spirit) . . ." This depends on an emendation of the manuscript. I am inclined to accept this second reading, but since it involves an unnecessary emendation have not printed it in the main text.

which follow them that this is found recorded in Matthew, and "in a certain place" "when he was praying . . . and he ceased." One of his disciples spoke to him, asking that he should teach them to pray "just as John taught his disciples" (Lk 11.1). For how can we accept that the same words should be spoken without any prior question and whilst set apart, and also publicly proclaimed at the request of a disciple. But perhaps it might be suggested that the prayers are equivalent in meaning, and are to be discussed as though they were one, once as in a private[44] communication and then at the request of another of the disciples, who surely was not present when he spoke what is recorded by Matthew, unless he had forgotten what had been spoken earlier. But it is better by far to reckon that the prayers are distinct, whilst having certain elements in common. When we searched in Mark, lest a prayer of similar meaning which had escaped our notice might be recorded there, we found not a trace of such a prayer to be present.

19

1   Now since, as we have said above, it is first necessary for the one who prays to be composed and disposed in a particular manner before praying, let us look at what our Savior says on this matter in the material immediately before the prayer that is in Matthew. They are as follow: "Whenever you pray, do not be like the hypocrites, who love to stand and pray in the synagogues and on the street corners, so that they may be observed by others. Truly I say to you: They have their reward. You, when you pray, go to your room and close the door, and pray to your Father who is hidden. And your Father, who

[44]The word translated "set apart" above and "private" here is a rare word and much prone to emendation, in particular as the manuscript has a different reading on each occasion. The two words must surely be the same. This reading is accepted on the basis that there is an implied contrast between the private setting in which Matthew's version of the prayer is delivered, and the public setting of Luke's account. Other possible readings are "in an extended speech" or "in the manner of a command."

sees what is hidden, shall reward you. Do not babble when you pray, as do the gentiles, for they think that they shall be heard because of their verbiage. You should not be like them, for your Father knows what need you have before you ask. Therefore you should pray in this way . . ." (Mt 6.5–9).

2   Our Savior appears frequently to take a stand against the love of glory as a passion that leads to destruction, just as he does here when he warns against hypocrisy on the occasion of prayer. For it is hypocrisy to desire human admiration for one's piety, rather than to seek communion with God.[45] We should remember the saying: "How can you believe when you receive human glory, and do not seek the glory which comes from the one who is alone God?" (Jn 5.44) We should despise all human glory, even should it be considered to have been honorably gained, and should seek the proper and true glory which is from him who alone gives glory to the one who is deserving of glory, who gives this glory in a manner fitting to himself and beyond the deserving of whomever receives it. Even should an act be considered honorable and praiseworthy, it is corrupted when performed so that we might receive human glory or so that we might be seen by people (Mt 6.2, 5), and on this account no kind of reward is forthcoming from God.

For every word of Jesus is truthful, and should we be pressed we might admit that it is all the more truthful when it is spoken with his accustomed oath. And of those who appear to do good for their neighbor for the sake of human glory, or who pray "in the synagogues and at the street corners" so that they might be visible to people he says: "Truly I tell you, they have received their reward" (Mt 6.5). For just as, according to Luke, the rich man enjoyed good things in his mortal lifetime, and so was prevented from receiving them after this present life, so whoever receives his reward, insofar as he has not sown for the spirit but for the flesh, shall reap destruction, and shall not reap eternal life either in his giving or in his

---

[45]The words "with God" are added following a suggestion of Anglus.

prayers (cf. Gal 6.8). It is sowing for the flesh when one gives alms in the synagogues and in the streets, with a trumpeting before one to court human admiration, as it is to love to stand praying in the synagogues and at the street corners in order to give a display of piety and to be considered saintly by the onlookers.

3   Indeed anyone who travels along the wide and spacious path which leads to destruction, which is not straight or direct but crooked and cornered throughout (for its straightness is all but broken up) has set his foot on it no less than those who pray at the street corners, not on one alone but, through love of pleasure, on several streets. In them there are those who are "humanly perishing" (Ps 81.7) because, having fallen away from their divinity, they are glorifying and blessing those whom they consider to be practicing piety[46] in the streets. There are always many who seem, when they pray, to be lovers of pleasure rather than lovers of God (2 Tim 3.4), who in the midst of their drinking parties and in their cups are drunk in their prayer. They are indeed standing at street corners to pray. For whoever lives a life of pleasure loves the spacious way, and has fallen away from the narrow and confined way of Jesus Christ, which has neither deviation nor the slightest turn.

20

1   If indeed there is a distinction between the church and the synagogue—I use the term "church" strictly, to mean that which is without spot or wrinkle or anything of the kind (Eph 5.27), which is holy and blameless, into which nobody born of a harlot may enter, nor any eunuch, nor anyone emasculated (Deut 23.1), nor an Egyptian, nor an Edomite, though their offspring of the third generation might join the church with some difficulty (Deut 23.7–8), nor a Moabite nor an Ammonite, except the tenth generation be completed and the age brought to an end (Deut 23.3), and by synagogue

---

[46]The manuscript has "practicing *im*piety" here, though the vast majority of editors emend the text.

I mean that built by the centurion in the days before the coming of Jesus, when witness had not been borne that he had faith such as the Son of God found not even in Israel (Mt 8.10)—then whoever enjoys praying in the synagogues is not far removed from the street corners. But the saint is not of this kind. For rather than enjoying prayer he loves it, and he does not pray in the synagogues but in the churches, and not on street corners but in the straightness of the narrow and confined way, and does not do so to be observed by people but in order to appear before the Lord God. For a male is the one who perceives "the acceptable year of the Lord" (Lk 4.19), who keeps the commandment that states: "Three times each year should every male appear before the Lord God" (Deut 16.16).

2   We should pay careful attention to the term "appear," for nothing that is merely apparent is worthy, since it seems to exist but does not actually do so, deceiving sense-perception and not giving a true or accurate representation.[47] For just as actors playing in the theater are not what they say they are, nor is their appearance like that of the character masks which they wear,[48] so all those who put on an outward show of goodness to be observed are not righteous, but are acting the part of righteousness, and are acting in a theater of their own, namely the synagogues and the street corners. Whoever is not an actor, but has put off all that is alien, who rehearses to make himself pleasing in a theater vastly superior to any that has been mentioned, goes to his own room, where his riches are stored, and locks his treasury of wisdom and knowledge behind him. He does not recognize the outside world, he pays no attention to anything outside, but shuts up every door of the senses, so that the world of the senses should not distract, nor his mind receive any impression from sense-perception, praying to the Father who neither shuns nor deserts such a secret place but dwells there together with the only-begotten

---

[47]This is the fundamental Platonic division between that which truly is, and is perceived by the mind, and those things that are impermanent and apparent which is the world perceived by the senses.

[48]Actors in the ancient world wore masks to represent their characters.

one. For he says: "I and the Father will come to him and make our home with him" (Jn 14.23). So it is clear that should we pray in this way we shall plead not only with a God who is righteous but with a father who does not desert his children and who is present with them in secret, who looks upon and increases the contents of the storeroom, should we only shut its door.

21

1   When we pray let us not babble, but speak with godliness. We babble when, without being self-aware or watching the words which we are offering up in prayer, we speak of corruptible deeds, or words, or thoughts, which are mean and reprehensible, which are alien to the incorruption of the Lord. Whoever babbles in praying is already in a worse condition than those in the synagogues of whom we have already spoken, and on a path even more ruinous than those who are at the street corners, for not a vestige is left even of the outward appearance of goodness. For, according to the saying of the Gospel, only the heathens babble, and in their requests they have no notion of what is great or heavenly, but the only prayer which they offer concerns bodily and external matters. So whoever asks inferior things from the one who is in the heavens and who dwells above the heights of the heavens is to be likened to the babbling heathen.

2   Now whoever is verbose is a babbler, and whoever is a babbler is verbose. For there is no unity in material or in bodies, for every supposed unity has lost its unity by being split up and disintegrated and divided into many. For the good is one but the shameful are many. Truth is one, but falsehoods are many, and true righteousness is one, but there are many bodily dispositions that simulate it. And the wisdom of God is one, but the wisdoms of this age, and the rulers of this age (1 Cor 2.6), enfeebled though they are, are many. The Word of God is one, but the words that are alien to God are many. For this reason nobody shall avoid sin through verbosity (Prov 10.19), and nobody who thinks that he will be heard through verbosity can be

heard. And so our prayers should not be comparable to the babblings or the verbosity of the heathen, or whatever it is that they do in the likeness of a serpent (Ps 57.5), for the God of the saints, as a father, knows his children's needs, since such things are worthy of his paternal knowledge. Anyone who is ignorant of God is ignorant of the things of God, and ignorant of the things that are necessary; what he reckons as necessary are the wrong things. But whoever has contemplated the better and more divine things, which are necessary to him, will obtain the objects of his contemplation, for they are known of God, and are known to the Father even before they are requested.

Now that we have said this about the preamble to the Prayer according to Matthew, let us consider what the Prayer teaches us.

22

1 "Our Father who are in the heavens." A careful examination of what is called the Old Testament is worthwhile, in order to discern whether anybody is to be found in it addressing their prayer to God as Father. For although I have made such an examination to the best of my ability I have yet to find any. This is not to say that God is not said to be a father, or that those who are accounted as believers are not called sons of God, but that boldness of speech in prayer which is revealed by the Savior in addressing God as "Father" I have yet to find. That God is said to be a father, and that those who have approached the word of God are described as sons, is frequently observable, as in Deuteronomy: "You have forsaken God who begot you, and you have forgotten God who nourished you" (Deut 32.18). And again: "Is he not your father who begot you and made you and created you?" (Deut 32.6) And again: "Sons, in whom there is no faith" (Deut 32.20). And in Isaiah: "I have begotten and raised up children, and they have rejected me" (Is 1.2). And in Malachi: "A son shall honor his father, and a slave his master. And if I am a father, where is my glory: and if I am a master, where is the fear due to me?" (Mal 1.6).

2   And so, even if God is termed "father," and those begotten by
the word through their faith in him are called "sons," nonetheless a
firm and abiding sonship is not to be discerned among the ancient
people. Moreover, the passages which we have adduced point to the
subjection of those who are called sons since, according to the apostle, "The heir, as long as he is a child, is no different from a slave, even
if he be master of all, for until the time appointed by the father he is
under tutors and governors" (Gal 4.1–2). And the fullness of time
comes with the advent of Our Lord Jesus Christ, when those who so
desire receive adoption, as Paul teaches in these words: "You have not
received the spirit of subjection to fear, but you have received the
Spirit of adoption, in which we cry out: 'Abba, Father.'" And in the
Gospel according to John: "To as many as received him, he gave
power to become children of God, to those who believe in his name"
(Jn 1.12). And in the general letter of John, we learn of those who are
begotten of God that "whoever is begotten of God does no wrongdoing, because his seed remains in him; and because he is begotten
of God he is unable to do wrong" (1 Jn 3.9).

3   And yet, should we consider the meaning of what is written in
Luke: "When you pray, say 'Father,'" we should be cautious of
addressing such an expression to him unless we have become genuine sons, lest we become liable to a charge of impiety in addition to
our other sins. What I mean is this. In the first letter to the Corinthians Paul says: "Nobody can say 'Jesus is Lord' except in the Holy
Spirit, and nobody who speaks in the Spirit of God says: 'Jesus be
cursed'" (1 Cor 12.3). Here he identifies Holy Spirit and the Spirit of
God. What is meant by saying "'Jesus is Lord' in the Holy Spirit"
is not altogether clear, since the expression is employed by thousands of hypocrites and yet more heterodox, and sometimes even by
demons who are overcome by the power that is in the name. Nobody
would venture to suggest that any of these is saying that Jesus is Lord
"in the Holy Spirit," and we would be hard put to show that they
indeed say that Jesus is Lord, for only those who say the words "Jesus
is Lord" with the purpose of serving the word of God [are saying

them fitly] when they address none other as Lord in anything that they do.[49] And if it be these who say "Jesus is Lord," perhaps we might say that anyone who sins is cursing the divine Word through his transgression, shouting "Jesus be cursed" through what he does. Thus, just as somebody of a particular disposition says "Jesus is Lord" and somebody of the opposite tendency says "Jesus be cursed," so it is that whoever is begotten of God and who does no wrongdoing, by sharing in the seed of God which diverts him from any wrongdoing, is saying through his conduct: "Our Father who are in the heavens." And the Spirit himself bears witness together with their spirit that they are children of God, and heirs, and joint heirs with Christ, since having suffered together with him they have the blessed hope of being glorified together with him (Rom 8.16–17). And in order that they should not say "Our Father" half-heartedly, the heart, which is the font and origin of good works, believes "for righteousness" alongside their works, and the mouth confesses salvation in harmony with them (Rom 10.10).

4   So then, their every work and word and thought, being conformed to himself by the only begotten Word, reflects the image of the invisible God and comes to be "in accordance with the image of the Creator" (Col 3.10), who causes the sun to rise on the wicked and the good and the rain to fall on the just and the unjust (Mt 5.45), so that the image of the heavenly one, who is himself the image of God, might be found in them. The saints are therefore an image of an image, that of the Son. They are stamped with sonship, and are conformed not only to the glorified body of Christ (Phil 3.21), but to the one who is in that body. They become conformed to the one who is in a glorified body, and are transformed through the renewal of their minds (Rom 12.2). And if it be these who in all things say: "Our Father, who are in the heavens" then it is clear that those who commit wrongdoing are, as John says in his general letter, "of the Devil, because the Devil sins from the beginning" (1 Jn 3.8). And just as the

---

[49]The words "are saying them fitly" are added to make translation feasible, following a suggestion of Anglus that words have been omitted.

seed of God remains in the one who is begotten of God, bringing about an inability to transgress in anyone who is conformed to the only begotten Word, so the seed of the devil is present in anyone who does commit wrongdoing and, inasmuch as it has dominance in the soul, it prevents its possessor from doing right. But since "the Son of God was revealed to undo the works of the Devil" (1 Jn 3.8) it is possible that the advent of the Word of God into the soul might undo the works of the devil, and root out the wicked seed within us, and that so we might become children of God.

5   We should not imagine that we are being taught to say these words at a certain fixed time for prayer. Rather, if we have understood what was said above concerning ceaseless prayer, may our entire life pray unceasingly by saying "Our Father who are in heaven." For our citizenship is in no way upon earth but is in every way in the heavens (Phil 3.20) which are the thrones of God, in that the Kingdom of God is established in all those who bear the image of the heavenly one (1 Cor 15.49) and have so themselves become heavenly.

23

1   When the Father of the saints is said to be "in the heavens," it is not to be supposed that he is circumscribed by corporeal shape, and that so he dwells "in the heavens," for if the heavens contain him it follows that God would be less than the heavens, whereas the ineffable power of his divinity entails our belief that all things are contained and held together by him. In general, those passages that are taken literally by simpler minds to mean that God is in space, such as those that follow from the Gospel according to John, are better to be interpreted in keeping with a mighty and spiritual conception of God. "Now before the feast of the Passover, Jesus, knowing that his hour had come and that he should depart this world and go to the Father, having loved his own who were in the world, loved them to the end" (Jn 13.1). And, a little later: "Knowing that the Father had

given all things into his hands, that that he had come from God and was going to God . . ." (Jn 13.3). And later: "You heard me say to you that I am departing and will come to you again. If you loved me you would rejoice that I am going to the Father" (Jn 14.28). And again, later: "Now I am returning to the one who sent me, and none of you has asked me 'Where are you going?'" (Jn 16.5) For if these passages are to be understood as referring to a place, then clearly the same applies to the passage: "Jesus answered and said to them: 'If anyone loves me he will keep my word, and my Father will love him, and we will come to him and make our home with him'" (Jn 14.23).

2   Surely these words are not to be taken as indicating a change of place on the part of the Father and the Son toward the lover of the word of Jesus! In the same way the others are not to be interpreted spatially, but rather the Word of God comes down to be with us in terms of his proper dignity. And when he has been humbled by being among people he is said to pass from this world to the Father, so that we might look upon him perfected there, returning to his proper fullness after the emptiness which he had when he "emptied himself" (Phil 2.8). And so we, with him as our guide, shall attain completion and shall be delivered from all emptiness. And so let the Word of God depart toward the one who sent him, leaving the world behind and going to the Father, as we seek to understand the words at the end of the Gospel according to John, "do not touch me, for I have not ascended to the Father," in a mystical sense, thinking of the ascension of the Son to the Father with sanctified insight as an ascension of the mind rather than of the body.

3   To link these points with "Our Father, who are in the heavens" was, I think, necessary for the sake of removing the degraded conception of God held by those who think that he is "in the heavens" in a spatial sense, and lest anybody say that God is in a material space. For it follows on from this that he is corporeal, from which derisive doctrines follow, namely that he is divisible and material and corruptible, for every body is divisible and material and corruptible. Or else let them tell us, not on the basis of simple intuition

but stating it in a way that demonstrates clear comprehension, how it is possible for material to be otherwise.[50]

Yet since, even before the bodily advent of Christ, there are many statements which appear to state that God is in corporeal space, it does not seem to me irrelevant to discuss some of them in order to do away with any hesitation on the part of those who, because they know no better, confine God, who is above all things, into a narrow and restricted space of their own imagining. First of all, in Genesis, it says: "Adam and Eve heard the voice of God walking in the garden in the cool of the evening. And Adam and his wife hid from the face of the Lord God in the midst of the trees in the garden" (Gen 3.8). To those who are unwilling to enter the treasury of the passage, who will not even knock at its door, will I put this question: can they demonstrate that the Lord God, who fills the heaven and the earth, who uses heaven as a throne (in a material sense, they must presume) and the earth as a footstool for his feet (Is 66.1), is contained by a place which, by comparison with the heaven and the earth, is so narrow, and yet that this garden (which they must suppose to be corporeal) is not filled with God but is so much greater in its size than he that it can contain him walking in it, so that the sound of his footfalls is audible? It is yet more absurd that, on this interpretation, Adam and Eve should, out of fear of God through their transgression, hide themselves "from the face of God in the midst of the trees in the garden." For it does not say that they simply wished to hide, but that they actually hid. How then is it, according to their view, that God speaks to Adam and asks: "Where are you?"

4   These matters we have discussed at greater length in examining the contents of the book of Genesis,[51] and so it is sufficient here to recall what is said by God in Deuteronomy, "I shall dwell among

---

[50]That God is a corporeal being was a doctrine held by the stoics, though they would define this as the purest of corporeal matter. Cf. Aristotle *Organon* 1.1, for the idea of the limitation of bodies to which Origen refers here.

[51]See the introduction for the relevance of this passage to the dating of *On Prayer*.

them and I shall walk among them," rather than disregard such an important question altogether. For his walk among the saints is much like his walking in the garden, since every sinner hides from God and flees his governance and avoids his presence.[52] In this way Cain, likewise, "departed from the presence of God and dwelt in the land of Nod, opposite Eden" (Gen 4.16). And just as he dwells in the saints, so he dwells in heaven, whether this be in every saint who bears the image of the heavenly one (1 Cor 15.49), or in Christ, in whom all those being saved are lights and stars of heaven, or whether he dwells there because of the saints who dwell in heaven, in accordance with the verse: "I have lifted up my eyes to you who dwell in heaven" (Ps 122.1). And yet the verse in Ecclesiastes, "do not rush to give utterance to speech before God, because God is in heaven above and you are on the earth below" (Eccl 5.2) serves to indicate the distance which separates those who are in the body of humiliation from those angels who are exalted with the help of the word, and from the powers of holiness, and from Christ himself. For it is not unreasonable that he should properly be the throne of his Father, and that he should allegorically be called "heaven" while his church should be termed "earth" and "a footstool for his feet."

5   We have cited a few statements from the Old Testament which are considered to represent God in a location so that, insofar as we have received the ability, we might persuade the reader at all times to hear the divine Scriptures in a loftier and more spiritual sense whenever they seem to teach that God is in a location. It was appropriate to link this topic with "Our Father, who are in the heavens" since this sets apart the essence of God from all begotten beings. On these, which do not participate [in the essence of divinity][53] there comes a certain glory from God, and power from him, and, so to speak, an outflowing of divinity.

---

[52]The manuscript reads: "avoids his bold speech," and the text is emended following a suggestion of Bentley and Delarue.

[53]The phrase "the essence of divinity" is to be understood and is editorially supplied here.

24

1   "Let your name be hallowed." Whether this indicates that the petition being made has not yet come about, or whether it asks that, having come about, it should not pass away but should be maintained,[54] it is clear from the language here that the hallowing of the name of the Father has not yet occurred, and so we are commanded, at least according to Matthew and Luke, to say: "Let your name be hallowed." But you might say: "How can a human being request that the name of God be hallowed as though it were not hallowed already?" We should explore the meaning of the "name" of the Father and what its hallowing might mean.

2   Now a name is a summary designation indicative of the proper quality of the thing named. Thus the apostle Paul has proper quality, that of his soul, which is of a certain kind; that of his mind, which contemplates particular things, and that of his body, which is of a certain kind. Now what is peculiar to these properties and not shared by anybody else is designated by the name "Paul," for there is no being in existence identical with Paul. But in the case of persons whose particular qualities, so to speak, alter, their names, according to Scripture, are quite rightly altered. Thus when the quality of Abram altered, he was called "Abraham," and in the case of Simon he was called "Peter," and in the case of Saul, the persecutor of Jesus, he was called "Paul." But in the case of God, insofar as he is himself unchangeable, and is eternally unalterable, the name that, so to speak, he bears is one, that which is mentioned in Exodus, "He who is," or words to that effect (Ex 3.14). Therefore, since everyone has conceived some notion of God, having in our minds something concerning him, though not all conceive of what he is, for few indeed, indeed we should say the fewest of the few, grasp his holiness[55] in

---

[54]The sentence here has been emended following Bentley and Delarue. The manuscript is incomprehensible, and all editors have been obliged to attempt some emendation.

[55]Bentley and Delarue emend this word to "individuality."

every respect, we are very properly taught a conception of him as holy, in order that we might perceive his holiness as creating, providing, judging, electing, abandoning, welcoming, rejecting: rewarding those who are so worthy and punishing each according to his deserving.

3   For in these and similar ways the particular quality of God, which I consider to be "the name of God," is, so to speak, expressed in the Scriptures. So in Exodus: "Do not take the name of the Lord your God in folly" (Ex 20.7). And in Deuteronomy: "Let my utterance be anticipated like rain, let my words descend like dew, like showers upon the fields and like snow upon the grass, because I have called the name of the Lord" (Deut 32.2–3). And in Psalms: "They shall remember your name in every generation and for ever" (Ps 44.18). Whoever thinks of God in an unsuitable manner takes the name of the Lord God "in folly," whereas whoever is able to utter words like rain, which work together with those who are listening so that their souls bear fruit, and who speaks words of exhortation like dew, who, in the torrent of his edifying words, brings his hearers a beneficial shower or most effectual snow, is able to do so by the means of having in mind his need of God to make perfect, and calling to his assistance the one who is truly able to supply what was mentioned. Everyone who truly penetrates the things of God remembers them rather than learns them, even should he reckon that he has heard them from somebody, or think that he has found the mysteries of religion by discovery.[56]

4   Just as anyone who prays asking that God's name be hallowed should consider what is said here, so in Psalms it is said: "Let us exalt his name together" (Ps 33.4), where the prophet enjoins us to attain the true and exalted understanding of the particular quality of God with harmony, being of one mind and of one knowledge. When one has participated in an outflowing of divinity, having been lifted up

---

[56]Here Origen is assuming that we are eternal souls, and therefore that the Platonic theory of recollection, outlined in the *Meno*, can be brought to bear upon the question of religious learning.

by God and having overpowered his foes, so that they are unable to rejoice over his fall, and so exalts the very power of God in which he has participated, this is exalting the name of God together. This is shown in the twenty-ninth Psalm, when it says: "I shall exalt you, Lord, because you have lifted me up and have not allowed my foes to rejoice over me" (Ps 29.2). A person exalts God when he has dedicated to him a dwelling place within himself, and so the title of the Psalm runs: "A Psalm sung for the dedication of the house of David."

5   Further it is to be observed with regard to the clause "Let your name be hallowed" and what follows, that all is in the imperative mood, that the translators frequently made use of imperatives rather than optatives, as in the Psalms: "Let lying lips, which speak lawlessness against the righteous, be put to silence" (Ps 30.19) instead of "may . . . be put to silence," and, in the one hundred and eighth Psalm, concerning Judas (for the entire Psalm is a petition regarding Judas, that these things would befall him): "Let the money-lender seek out all his possessions, let there be none to assist him" (Ps 108.11–12). But Tatian, failing to perceive that "Let there be" does not always signify the optative, but sometimes the imperative, has proposed the most blasphemous reading of God's saying: "Let there be light" (Gen 1.3). He suggests that rather than commanding light He prayed for it, since, as he says in his godless thinking: "God was in darkness."

In response to him we might ask how he intends to take "Let the earth put forth grass" (Gen 1.11) and "Let the waters under the heaven be gathered together" (Gen 1.9) and "Let the waters put forth living creatures which creep" (Gen 1.20) and "Let the earth put forth a living being" (Gen 1.24). Is it then for the sake of standing on firm ground that he prays that the waters under the heaven be gathered into one place? Or is it for the sake of partaking in the things that the earth puts forth that he prays for the earth to put forth? And what need, like our need of light, does he have of creatures of the sea, or birds, or of the dry land, so that he has to pray for them? But should he admit that it is absurd for God to pray for these things, which are expressed through the imperative, how can he not say that the same is true of the saying "let there be light," namely that it is said not as a prayer in the optative but as a command in the imperative.

I felt obliged, given that the prayer is expressed in imperatives, to make some reference to his interpretation on behalf of those who have been misled into accepting his blasphemous teaching, some of whom we have previously met.[57]

25

1 "Let your Kingdom come." If, according to the word of our Lord and Savior, the Kingdom of God does not come with observable signs, and people will not say "Here it is!" or "There it is," but the Kingdom of God is within us (Lk 17.20–21), then it is clear that whoever prays for the coming of the Kingdom of God is praying most blessedly for the springing up and the bearing of fruit and the perfection of the Kingdom within himself (for the word is very near, it is in our mouth and in our heart [Deut 30.14]). Moreover, every saint is governed by God and is obedient to the spiritual laws of God who dwells within him as in a well-ordered city. So the Father is present to him, and Christ reigns together with the Father in the soul which has been perfected in accordance with the saying of which I made mention shortly before:[58] "We will come to him and make our home with him" (Jn 14.23). I think that the meaning of "the Kingdom of God" is the happy settlement of our governing faculty,[59] and the ordering of wise reflections, and that the Kingdom of Christ is the issue of words which bring salvation to those who hear them, and the practice of acts of righteousness and of the other virtues, for the Son of God is both word and righteousness.

But every sinner is tyrannized by the ruler of this present age, since every sinner is claimed by this present wicked age, and yields

---

[57]Tatian was a Christian teacher in Syria during the second century. Origen also deals with Tatian's interpretation of this saying at *Against Celsus* 6.672.

[58]At 20.2 and 23.1.

[59]*Hēgemonikon*, the part of the mind which gives rise to action.

himself not to the one who "gave himself for us sinners, to deliver us from this present wicked age," delivering us "in accordance with the will of God our Father" (as it is stated in the letter to the Galatians [Gal 1.4]). Whoever is tyrannized by the ruler of this age by reason of voluntary sin is governed likewise by sin. Therefore we are commanded by Paul no longer to be subject to the sin which desires to govern us, and in these words we are directed: "Do not let sin govern in our mortal body, so that we should be subject to its urgings" (Rom 6.12).

2   But somebody will object, with regard to both clauses, namely "let your name be hallowed" and "Let your Kingdom come," saying that anybody who prays is praying in the expectation of being heard, and that, should he be heard, then, in accordance with what was said before, it is plain that the name of God will be hallowed for him and that the Kingdom of God will be established in him. But if this occurs, how can he continue with propriety to pray for things which are already present as though they were not so, saying "let your name be hallowed, let your Kingdom come." If this is so, it is more fitting not to say "let your name be hallowed, let your Kingdom come."

To this we should reply that somebody who prays for a word of knowledge and a word of wisdom may properly continue to pray for these things since, as his prayer is heard, he will receive fuller ideas of wisdom and knowledge. He knows only "in part" the extent to which he may at present obtain such things, but then the perfection, which does away with what is partial, shall be revealed, and the mind shall confront its objects face to face, distinct from sense-experience (cf. 1 Cor 13.9–10). And so perfection in the hallowing of the name of God in each of us and in the establishment of his Kingdom is impossible until perfection in knowledge and wisdom, and perhaps the other virtues, is brought about. We are on a pilgrimage toward perfection if we stretch out toward the things ahead of us, forgetful of whatever is behind. The consummation of the Kingdom of God will be established within us who advance ceaselessly when that which is spoken by the apostle is fulfilled, when Christ, having subdued all his foes, delivers the Kingdom to God, the Father, so that God may be all in all (1 Cor 15.24, 28). Therefore, with a disposition made divine by the Word, praying ceaselessly, let us say to our Father who is in the heavens, "Let your name be hallowed, let your Kingdom come."

3   Moreover, we should understand with regard to the Kingdom of God that just as there is no fellowship between righteousness and injustice, and no communion between light and darkness, and no agreement between Christ and Belial (2 Cor 6.14–15), so the kingdom of sin cannot co-exist with the Kingdom of God. If, then, we desire that God reign within us, sin should have no sovereignty within our mortal bodies (Rom 6.12), and we should not obey its commands to do the works of the flesh or its provocation of the soul to deeds that are alien to God. Rather we should "mortify our members which are on the earth" (Col 3.5) and bring forth the fruit of the Spirit, so that the Lord may walk in us as in a spiritual garden as he alone reigns within us, with his Christ seated at the right hand of that spiritual power which we have prayed to receive, so seated until all his foes within us become a footstool for his feet (Ps 109.1) and every principality and authority and power within us is effaced. It is indeed possible that these things may occur within each of us, and that the last enemy, death, may be destroyed (1 Cor 15.26), so that Christ within us might say: "Where, death, is your sting? Where, hell, is your victory?" (1 Cor 15.55). So now whatever is corruptible within us should put on holiness and incorruption, in chastity and purity, and whatever is mortal should wrap itself in our ancestral immortality since death has been undone, so that, as God reigns within us, even now we may enjoy the good things of restoration and resurrection.

26

1   "Let your will be done—as in heaven so also on earth." After "Let your Kingdom come" Luke passes over this clause and continues with "Give us our supersubstantial bread daily." Let us examine,

then, these words, which Matthew alone sets down, in the light of what precedes them. We who pray while still on earth, being mindful that in heaven the will of God is done by all the inhabitants of the heavens, should pray that in like manner the will of God should be done on earth by us as it is by them. This will come about when we do nothing contrary to his will. And when the will of God as it is in heaven is upheld by us who are on the earth then we shall be made like those who are in heaven, bearing, like them, the image of the heavenly one (1 Cor 15.41), inheriting the Kingdom of the heavens while those who follow us on earth pray that they may in turn become like us who are in heaven.

2   It is indeed possible that the words which are only in Matthew, "as in heaven—so also on earth" might be taken as common to all, so that what we are directed to say in our prayer is this: "Let your name be hallowed, as in heaven—so also on earth. Let your Kingdom come, as in heaven—so also on earth. Let your will be done, as in heaven—so also on earth." For the name of God is hallowed by those in heaven and the Kingdom is present for them and the will of God is done in them. All of these are lacking to those of us who are on the earth, but we may nonetheless attain them through making ourselves fit to be heard by God with regard to them all.

3   The phrase: "Let your will be done—as in heaven, so also on earth" might lead somebody to enquire how the will of God is done even in heaven, where there is spiritual wickedness, on which account even in heaven the sword of God will drink deeply (Eph 6.12; Is 34.5). So if we pray that the will of God be done on earth, just as it is in heaven, might we not unwittingly pray that the very opposite remain on earth, since it is from heaven that so much comes that is bad on earth as a result of being overcome by the spiritual wickedness which derives from the heavenly places? Anybody who interprets "heaven" allegorically as Christ, and "earth" as the church (for what throne is as worthy of the Father as Christ, and what better footstool for the feet of God than the church?) will so readily solve the problem by stating that everybody in the church should pray that

they might receive the Father's will as Christ received it, for he came to do the will of his Father and completed it perfectly. For it is possible to be so joined to him as to become one spirit with him, and so to receive the will of God so that just as it is perfected in heaven so it may be perfected on earth also. For according to Paul "Whoever is joined to the Lord is one spirit" (1 Cor 6.17). And I believe that this interpretation will not lightly be set aside by anyone who gives it careful consideration.

4   By further objection we might cite what is said by the Lord to the eleven disciples at the conclusion of this Gospel after the resurrection: "All authority is given to me, both on heaven and on earth" (Mt 28.18). Already having authority over whatever is in heaven he declares that he has received it over whatever is on earth. For whatever is in heaven was already enlightened by the Word, and at the consummation of the world those which are on earth are brought to completion in heaven through the authority which is given to the Son of God, in imitation of those things over which the Savior received authority. So to speak he wishes to receive his disciples, through their prayers, as fellow-laborers on behalf of the Father so that, just as whatever is in heaven has been set in order by truth and reason, so whatever is on earth might be brought to completion by reason of the authority which he received "as in heaven, so also on earth," and thus that he might lead those who have submitted to his authority to a conclusion rich in blessing. Whoever desires that "heaven" should stand for the Savior and "earth" for the church, asserting that heaven is "the firstborn of all creation" (Col 1.15) on whom the Father reposes as on a throne, would find that it is the man whom He put on, who was made fit for this authority through his humbling of himself and through his obedience even to death (cf. Phil 2.8), who says, after his resurrection: "All authority is given to me, both on heaven and on earth." For the man who is in the Savior receives authority over whatever is in heaven, which is the proper domain of the only-begotten one, so that the communion between them might be perfected. For this humanity is mingled and united with his divinity.

5   Yet although the second interpretation does not solve the issues mentioned before, regarding how the will of God should be in heaven when there are spiritual forces of wickedness in the heavenly places which wrestle against those who are on the earth, it might be possible to answer the questions in the following manner. Just as somebody who is still on earth may have citizenship in the heavens, not by location but by desire, and may lay up treasure in heaven, and may have a heart in heaven, and may bear the image of the heavenly One, and so be no longer of the earth, or of the world below, but of heaven and of the heavenly world that is better than this, so the spiritual forces of wickedness, although they still dwell in the heavenly places, have their citizenship on earth and, through their struggling and plotting against humanity, are laying up treasure on earth, and bear the image of the earthly one, which is the "beginning of the Lord's creation, made to be mocked by the angels" (Job 40.14), and so are not heavenly, and have no home in the heavens by virtue of their vicious disposition. Accordingly, whenever "Let your will be done—as in heaven, so also on earth" is said, we should not reckon that those who, by their presumption, have fallen with the one who fell from heaven like lightning, are in heaven.

6   And perhaps, when our Savior says that we should pray that the will of the Father should be done on earth, as it is in heaven, he is not by any means demanding that prayer should be made for what is spatially situated on earth, that this should be made like to whatever is spatially situated in heaven, but rather his prescription of prayer is the result of his desire that whatever is on earth, that is whatever is inferior and conformed to the earthly, should be made like the good, and have citizenship in heaven, and have all become "heaven." For the sinner, wherever he may be, is "earth" and, unless he repent, will return to his kindred earth in some way or other. Whereas whoever does the will of God, and is not disrespectful of the spiritual laws of salvation, is "heaven." And so, even if we are still "earth" on account of sin, let us pray that the will of God might be spread out over us for our restoration, just as it reached those before us who are

becoming heaven, or who are already so. And if we are already accounted by God not as "earth" but as "heaven," let us ask that the will of God be fulfilled on earth, by which I mean amongst inferior things, as it is in heaven, so that, as one might say, in earth's heaven-making there shall be earth no longer as all things become heaven. For if the will of God, according to this interpretation, be done on earth, the earth shall remain earth no longer.

We may clarify this with a further illustration. Should the will of God be done among the dissipated as it is among the restrained, then the dissipated will become restrained, or if the will of God be done among the unrighteous as among the just, so the unrighteous will become just. And so, if the will of God be done "as in heaven— so also on earth," so shall we all become heaven. For whereas the flesh, which avails nothing (Jn 6.63), and blood, which is akin to it, "cannot inherit the Kingdom of God" (1 Cor 15.50), they might be said to inherit should they be transformed from flesh and earth and dirt and blood into heavenly substance.

27

1   "Give us today our supersubstantial bread," or, as Luke has it: "Give us our supersubstantial bread daily." Since some assume that we are being charged to pray for corporeal bread, we should set forth the truth concerning the supersubstantial bread in order to refute their false opinions. We should say to them: "How is it that the one who says that we should make our request with regard to heavenly and great matters now demands that we should offer request with regard to something earthly and petty, as though he had forgotten what he had taught with regard to such matters? For the bread which is assimilated to our flesh is not heavenly, nor is asking for it a request for something great.

2   But we shall explain these words by extensive citation, following the teacher himself in his teaching concerning the bread. According to John he said to those who had come to Capernaum to seek

him: "Truly, truly I say to you, you seek me not because you saw the signs but because you ate of the loaves and were satiated" (Jn 6.26). For whoever eats of the loaves that are blessed by Jesus and is filled with them seeks the more accurately to comprehend the Son of God and hastens toward him. And so he rightly directs them: "Do not work for food which perishes, but for food which continues into eternal life, which the son of man will give you" (Jn 6.27). And when his hearers enquired into this and said: "What should we do to perform the works of God?" Jesus answered them and said: "This is the work of God, that you should believe in the one whom he sent" (Jn 6.28–29). As it is written in the Psalms, referring to the diseased: God "sent his Word and healed them" (Ps 106.20). Those who put their trust in this word are they who perform the works of God, which is the food that continues into eternal life. Again he says: "My Father gives you the true bread from heaven. The bread of God is that which comes down from heaven and gives life to the world" (Jn 6.32–33). And the bread is that which gives nourishment to the true humanity, which is made in the image of God, and so whoever is so nourished grows into the likeness of the creator. What is more nourishing to the soul than reason? And what is more precious to the mind of whoever receives it than the wisdom of God? And what is more agreeable to the rational nature than truth?

3   Should anyone suggest an objection to this, saying that he would not have taught that we should ask for supersubstantial bread as though it were something other than himself, it should be noted that, also in the Gospel according to John, he gives discourse sometimes as if it were something other than himself and sometimes as though he were himself the bread. So, as though referring to something else, in these words: "Moses gave you the bread from heaven, not the true bread, but my Father gives you the true bread from heaven" (Jn 6.32). And to those who said to him "give us this bread always" he says, as though of himself: "I am the bread of life. Whoever comes to me shall not go hungry, and whoever believes in me shall never thirst" (Jn 6.34–35). And a little later: "I am the living

bread which came down from heaven. If anyone eat of this bread, he shall live forever. And the bread which I shall give is my flesh, which I shall give on behalf of the life of the world" (Jn 6.51).

4   Since Scripture refers to all nourishment as "bread,"[60] as is clear from what is recorded of Moses, that he ate no bread and drank no water for forty days (Deut 9.9), and since the nourishing word is varied and diverse, for not all are able to receive sustenance from the solidity and strength of divine doctrines, he desires to supply nourishment fitting for the training of those who are nearer perfection as he says: "The bread which I shall give is my flesh, which I shall give on behalf of the life of the world" (Jn 6.51) and a little later: "Unless you eat the flesh of the son of man and drink his blood you shall have no life in you. Whoever eats my flesh and drinks my blood has eternal life and I shall raise him on the last day. For my flesh is true food and my blood is true drink. Whoever eats my flesh and drinks my blood remains in me and I in him. Just as the living Father sent me, and I live through the Father, so whoever eats me shall live through me" (Jn 6.53–57). That is the true food, the flesh of Christ, which, being word, became flesh, in accordance with the statement: "And the Word was made flesh" (Jn 1.14). He "dwells among us" whenever we eat and drink him. And whenever it is distributed the saying "We looked upon his glory" is fulfilled. "This is the bread which came down from heaven, not like that which the ancestors ate, and died. Whoever eats this bread shall live for ever" (Jn 6.58).

5   Paul, moreover, in discussing this matter with "infant" Corinthians who walk "in human ways" says: "I fed you with milk, and not with solids, for you were not yet able. But you are still unable, for you are fleshly" (1 Cor 3.1–3). And in the letter to the Hebrews: "You have become like those whose need is milk, and not solid food. For whoever partakes of milk is incompetent in the word of righteousness, for he is an infant, whereas solid foods are for those who are mature, whose senses have been trained by experience in the discrimination

[60]Cf. *Commentary on John* 10.13.

of good and evil" (Heb 5.12–14). In my opinion the saying: "One believes that anything may be eaten, whereas the weak eats vegetables" (Rom 14.2) is not principally directed to corporeal food but to the words of God that nourish the soul. For the person who is of fullest faith and greatest maturity, who is denoted by the words "One believes that anything may be eaten," is able to digest everything, whereas somebody who is weaker and less developed, whom he intends to denote with "the weak eat vegetables," is contented with simpler teaching which does not bring about so much strength.

6   There is also Solomon's saying in Proverbs which teaches, I think, that the person who is incapable of the more vigorous and mightier teaching is, as long as there is no error in his thinking, better than anyone who, being better prepared, and sharper, tackles weightier matters yet fails to penetrate the peace and harmony underlying all things. His words are as follows: "Better a supper of vegetables with friendship and grace than a calf from the stall with enmity" (Prov 15.17). For we have often taken a plain and simple meal with a good conscience as guests of those who are unable to offer us anything better, and have done so with greater satisfaction than any elevation of words rising up against the knowledge of God, proclaiming, with apparent plausibility, teaching contrary to the Father of our Lord Jesus Christ, who gave us the law and the prophets.[61] In order, therefore, not to fall sick of soul for lack of nourishment, nor to die through famine of the Lord's word (cf. Am 8.11), let us, in fidelity to the teaching of our Savior, rightly believing and rightly living, ask the Father for the living bread, which is the same as the supersubstantial bread.[62]

7   We should now give consideration to the meaning of "supersubstantial" (*epiousios*). First of all we should note that the word

[61]The obvious target of these words is the Marcionites. If this is the case, then there is a certain irony, for the Marcionites were notable for the simplicity of their diet.

[62]For a discussion of the chapter thus far and its doctrine of nourishment, note Virginia L. Noel, "Nourishment in Origen's *On Prayer*" in R.J. Daly (ed.), *Origeniana Quinta* (Leuven: Peeters, 1992), 481–487.

"supersubstantial" (*epiousios*) is not employed by any of the Greek writers, nor by philosophers, nor by individuals in common usage, but seems to have been formed by the evangelists; at least Matthew and Luke concur in employing the term in an identical manner. Those who translated the Hebrew Scriptures have done something similar elsewhere; for what Greek ever used the expression "receive with your ears" or "hear ye up," instead of "lend an ear," or "listen!"[63] An expression of great similarity to *epiousios* is found in Moses' writings, as spoken by God: "You shall be my particular (*periousios*) people" (Ex 19.5). It seems to me that each of these words is derived from the word "essence" (*ousia*). The one denotes the bread that is conjoined with the divine essence, the other signifies the proximity of the people to the essence and their participation in it.

8   Now essence (*ousia*) is considered by those who assert that the principal underlying reality (*hypostasis*) is incorporeal properly to refer to incorporeal things; these are said to have permanence, and not to be subject to addition or to suffer subtraction. For this is a property of bodies; due to being in a state of flux they may grow or decay, and require support or nourishment from an external agent. If there is an occasion on which more is imported than seeps away, then growth occurs; but if there is less, then there is diminution. Should there perhaps be bodies that admit of no exterior support, one might say that they are in unmitigated diminution.

On the other hand there are those who hold that the essence of incorporeal things is secondary to that of bodies. They define essence in these terms: it is the primary matter out of which things which exist have their existence; or that it is the material of bodies through which they exist; or that it subsists in being named, and that things which have a name have essence; or that it is a primary

---

[63]A certain liberty in translation of this sentence is unavoidable. Origen alludes to the usage of the Septuagint. Thus Job 33.1 has *enōtizou*, whereas more natural Greek usage would be *eis ta ōta dexai*. Anglus points out, however, that *akoutisthēti*, the second unnatural usage to which Origen refers, translated here as "hear ye up," is not found within the Septuagint.

substrate without qualities; or that it is something unalterable of itself which admits all kinds of change and alteration; or that it is the underlying basis of anything which undergoes alteration and change. According to these thinkers essence (*ousia*) is inherently without quality and without form, nor does it have any size of its own, but it underlies[64] every quality as though it were a ground made ready for it. By "qualities" they distinctively mean what are commonly called the motivations and actions by which potentiality and actuality is brought about. They say that essence of itself has no participation in these qualities, yet by reason of its receptivity it is invariably inseparable from one of them, for it is absolutely receptive of every motivation of any agent bringing about either quality or alteration. For there is a force present with it which pervades the universe and acts as a cause for each of its qualities and activities. They say that it is completely alterable and completely divisible and that any essence might coalesce with any other essence, but by being united with it.[65]

9   What I have said in this exploration into the word "essence" (*ousia*), which was raised by the expressions "the supersubstantial (*epiousios*) bread" and "the particular (*periousios*) people," is intended to discern the meanings of "essence." We have seen that the bread for which we should ask is above all bread for the mind, so we must understand that the bread is related to this essence. And so, just as corporeal bread received into the body of the person who is being nourished is accepted by his essence, so the living bread which has come down from heaven is received into the mind and the soul of

[64]*hupokeitai* is read here, following Anglus, rather than *egkeitai*, which is the reading of the manuscript.

[65]In this section, Origen is contrasting the Platonic idea of reality, by which the only things which really exist (i.e., have essence, or *ousia*) are incorporeal ideas, of which everyday objects and experiences are imperfect manifestations, with the fundamentally Aristotelian idea of essence (*ousia*), which refers to corporeal objects and ascribes permanence not to an abstract idea of reality but to an underlying physical reality, of which everyday objects are all formed. Although this idea is founded in Aristotle, it was taken up in various ways by different schools of thought, prominent among whom were the Stoics.

whoever allows himself to receive nourishment from it, and imparts its own power to him. And thus it becomes the "supersubstantial" bread for which we ask. And again, just as whoever receives nourishment gains strength which varies in accordance with the nature of the food, whether it be solid and fit for athletes, or derived from milk or from vegetables, so it follows that whether the word of God be given as milk fit for children, or as vegetables fitting those who are unwell, or as meat suitable for those who are engaged in struggle, each of those who receives nourishment is able to accomplish whatever or to become whatever in accordance to the extent to which he has surrendered himself to the word. However, some of what is thought to be food is actually harmful, then there is food that causes disease, and some which is indigestible; by analogy, any of these may be applied to different doctrines that are thought to be nourishing. The "supersubstantial" bread, therefore, is that which corresponds most closely to the rational nature, and is related to its essence, bringing about health and well-being and strength in the soul and, since the word of God is immortal, communicating its own immortality to anyone who eats it.

10   This supersubstantial bread seems to me to be mentioned under another name in the Scripture—the tree of life; whoever stretches forth a hand and takes of it shall live forever (Gen 3.22). And this tree is called by a third name, "the wisdom of God," by Solomon, in these words: "She is a tree of life to all who reach out for her, and safe for all who lean on her as on the Lord" (Prov 3.18). And since the angels are also nourished by the wisdom of God, empowered for the completion of their particular tasks by their contemplation of the truth in wisdom, it is said in the Psalms that the angels receive nourishment, and that the people of God, who are styled Hebrews, share this with the angels and become, as it were, table-companions with the angels. This is the meaning of: "A human ate the bread of angels" (Ps 77.25). Let our mind be not so impoverished as to imagine that the Hebrews shared some kind of corporeal bread, such as that which, it is recorded, came down from heaven on those

who were departing from Egypt, with the angels who are the ministering spirits of God.

11   While we are exploring the supersubstantial bread and the tree of life and the wisdom of God and the common nourishment of humans and of angels, it is not inopportune to refer to the three men of whom it is written in Genesis that they turned off to Abraham and partook of three measures of flour kneaded into cakes (Gen 18.2–6). We may strip away at this, as in a figurative sense it shows that saints are able to share mental and rational nourishment not only with humans but with more divine powers, either to assist them or as a demonstration of the nourishment that they have been able to produce for themselves. The angels rejoice and are nourished by such a demonstration, and become the readier to cooperate in every way, to conspire in the comprehension of further and greater things on the part of the one who had caused them to rejoice and, so to speak, supplied them with such nourishing teaching that he had already prepared. If a human feeds angels, it is scarcely to be wondered at when even Christ admits that he stands at the door and knocks, that he may enter the home of whomsoever answers and dine with him on whatever is his (Rev 3.20), so that afterward he may himself bestow what is his to the person who first entertained the Son of God from what was his.

12   So, whoever partakes of the supersubstantial bread becomes a son of God through the strengthening of his heart; whereas whoever partakes of the dragon is nothing but a mental Ethiopian, himself changing, through the snares of the dragon, into a serpent, so that even should he say that he desires to be baptized he is reproached by the word and hears: "Serpents! Generations of vipers! Who warned you to flee from the wrath that is coming?" (Mt 3.7). And David says this about the body of the dragon on which the Ethiopians feast: "You crushed the heads of the dragons on the water, you break the dragon's head into pieces. You gave him as food to the peoples of Ethiopia" (Ps 73.13–14). But since the Son of God subsists essentially, and the adversary likewise, it should not seem strange

that they should each become nourishment for one or another person. So why do we hesitate to admit that, in respect of any of the powers, whether for the better or for the worse, and even in respect of human beings, each of us may derive nourishment from any of these? Indeed, when Peter was about to have fellowship with Cornelius the centurion and those who were gathered with him in Caesarea, and afterward to share the word of God with the gentiles, he saw a vessel from heaven "let down by its four corners" on which were "all kinds of quadrupeds and serpents and wild animals of the earth" (Acts 10.11–12). He is then commanded to get up, to slaughter and to eat. After he refused, and said: "You know that nothing common or unclean has ever entered my mouth" (Acts 11.8), he is charged that he should call no person common or unclean (Acts 10.28) since what has been cleansed by God should not be held common by Peter. The text says: "Do not hold as common what God has made clean" (Acts 10.15). Accordingly, the clean and unclean food that is distinguished according to the law of Moses by the names of many animals has reference to the different kinds of rational creatures. It is teaching that some are nourishing for us and that others are the opposite, unless God cleanses them all, or those of every kind, and makes them nourishing.

13   While this is indeed so, and while there is such variety in foods, the supersubstantial bread is that single food for which we should pray above all others mentioned. We should pray to be counted worthy of it and to be nourished by the Word who was with God in the beginning, and so to be made divine.

Somebody might say that "supersubstantial" (*epiousion*) is derived from "come upon" (*epieinai*), and that we are being commanded to ask for the bread which belongs to the age to come, that God should grant it to us even now, in anticipation, that what should be given us tomorrow be given us today. "Today" is thus understood to refer to the present age and "tomorrow" to the age to come. Although to the best of my judgment the former interpretation is better, let us proceed to examine "today," which is extant in Matthew at this point, or "daily" in Luke. It is the custom of the Scriptures frequently to call every age "today," as in: "He is the father of the Moabites to this very day" (Gen 19.37) and "He is the father of the Ammonites to this very day" and "this tale is told among the Jews until today" (Mt 28.15), and in the Psalms: "If you would hear his voice today, do not harden your hearts" (Ps 94.7–8). This is made very clear in Joshua, as it says: "Do not desert the Lord in these present days" (Josh 22.16–18). If "today" is all this age, is not "yesterday" the age that is passed? I have understood this to be the meaning in Psalms and of Paul in the Letter to the Hebrews. In Psalms it is thus: "A thousand years in your sight are like a day, like yesterday that has passed" (Ps 89.4). This is the much-discussed millennium—it is compared to yesterday rather than to today.[66] In the apostle it is written: "Jesus Christ, yesterday, and today, and for ever the same" (Heb 13.8). It is scarcely to be wondered at that an entire age for God is described as the span of a single day for us, indeed, I might suggest, as even less.

14   We may also enquire whether the words that direct feasts or assemblies in terms of days or months or seasons or years are to be applied to ages. For if the law is a shadow of the things which are to come about (Heb 10.1), its many sabbaths must of necessity be a shadow of many days, and the new moons markers of intervals of time, completed by some kind of conjunction of the moon, I know not what, with some sun. And if the first month, from the tenth day until the fourteenth (Ex 12.2–3, 6), and the feast of unleavened bread from the fourteenth until the twenty-first (Ex 12.18), contain a shadow of the things which are to come about, who is there who is wise and a friend of God to such an extent as to perceive which is the first of several months, and what is the tenth day, and so on?

---

[66]Origen so swats away the belief, widespread in early Christianity, that Christ would reign on earth for a thousand years. He dismisses the same doctrine in *On First Principles* 2. The doctrine was still being hotly discussed in Egypt at the time of Dionysius, who travelled to Arsinoe in middle Egypt to discuss the issue after the doctrine was espoused by the bishop Nepos (as told in Eusebius *Ecclesiastical History* 7.24).

And what need do I have to speak of the feast of the seven weeks (Deut 16.9) and of the seventh month (Lev 16.29), the new moon of which is a day of trumpets, and of which the tenth is a day of atonement (Lev 23.24–28)? These are known only to God who legislated them. Who has obtained the mind of Christ to such an extent that he is able adequately to comprehend the emancipation of Hebrew domestic slaves in the seventh years (Ex 21.2), and the release of debts (Lev 25.4–7), and the cessation of agriculture in the Holy Land (Deut 15.1)? And over and above the feast of seven years is that called the Jubilee (Lev 25.8). Nobody who has not contemplated the Father's will in the arrangement of all the ages in accordance with his unsearchable judgments and his impenetrable ways (Rom 11.33) may imagine its meaning with any clarity, or know the true fulfillment of these laws.

15   I have often experienced confusion in trying to reconcile two statements of the apostle with regard to how there can be a consummation of the ages, in which Jesus is revealed once only for the abolition of sins, if there are to be ages to come after this one. His statements are as follow. In Hebrews: "He has appeared now, once only, at the consummation of the ages, to abolish sin through his sacrifice" (Heb 9.26). In Ephesians: "That he might show, in the ages to come, the wealth of his grace through his kindness to us" (Eph 2.7). Hazarding a guess at such a matter I reckon that just as the consummation of the year is the final month, after which the beginning of another month comes about, so perhaps many ages make up a year of ages,[67] to which the present age provides a consummation, after which ages to come will arise, whose beginning is the age to come, and in those ages which are to come God will show the wealth of his grace through his kindness. The greatest of sinners, who has spoken ill against the Holy Spirit, is held fast by his sin throughout this entire present age. How he will be treated from the beginning to the end of that which is to come hereafter I do not know.[68]

[67]Cf. *Commentary on Matthew* 15.31.
[68]Cf. *On First Principles* 3.6.5–6.

16   When somebody has a vision of these matters, has perception of the week of ages, so he comes to contemplate a kind of holy Sabbath. He fixes in his mind on a month of ages, and so perceives the holy new moon of God, and on a year of ages, and so comes indeed to understand the feasts of the year, when every male must appear before the Lord God (Deut 16.16), and in the same way on the years of so many ages, so to comprehend the holy seventh year, and the seven times seven years of ages, and so he comes, through studying in this way, to sing a hymn to a lawgiver so mighty. How then can anyone undervalue even the slightest portion of an hour of the day of so great an age, rather than doing whatever is possible to receive the supersubstantial bread "daily," having by preparation here become worthy to gain it "today"? From what has been said already it is clear what "daily" means. For whoever prays to God, who is from infinity to infinity, not only for "today" but in some sense for what is "daily," will be able to receive from the one who is able to grant "much more than we can ask or conceive" (Eph 3.20), which, if I may speak with such exaggeration, are even beyond "what eye has not seen," and which are beyond "what human heart has conceived" (1 Cor 2.9).

17   These investigations seem to me to have been most necessary for the understanding of the expressions "today" and "daily" when we pray that the supersubstantial bread might be given us from his Father. If, according to the final book, when it says not "and give today the supersubstantial bread" but "Give us the supersubstantial bread daily," we examine the word "our," so we may enquire how this bread comes to be ours. However the apostle teaches that all things belong to the saints, whether life or death, or things present or things to come" (1 Cor 3.22). But there is no necessity to speak of this[69] at present.

---

[69]The words "of this" are editorial, and not in the manuscript. If the meaning of this section is obscure, that is because the text is so corrupt that it cannot readily be understood.

28

1   "And forgive us our debts, as we also have forgiven our debtors."
Or, as Luke has it, "And forgive us our sins, as we ourselves pardon
everyone indebted to us." The apostle also says, concerning debts:
"Pay your debts to all. To whom tribute is owed, tribute, to whom
fear is owed, fear, to whom tax is owed, tax, to whom honor is owed,
honor. Be indebted to nobody, except to each other for love" (Rom
13.7–8). We are therefore debtors not only in our duty of giving but
also in gentle speech, indeed we are obliged to have a disposition of
this nature toward one another. Since we owe this much we either
pay, and so fulfill the precepts of the divine law, or we do not pay, in
disregard of sound advice, and so remain indebted.

2   A like mind is to be had in regard to debts toward brothers or
sisters, whether those who are regenerate with us in Christ, understanding the terms in their religious sense, or those who share the
same father or mother with us. We also have certain obligations
toward fellow-citizens, and toward the human race in general, and
especially toward strangers and toward those who are old enough
to be our fathers, and another toward those whom we should right-
fully honor as sons or as brothers. Whoever, therefore, does not fulfill obligations owed toward brothers and sisters remains a debtor in
respect of what is undone. Likewise we, should we be found wanting with regard to what is due toward others from us in the humane
spirit of wisdom, our debt becomes the greater. Moreover, as regards
ourselves, we are indebted in a certain way in the use of our body, in
not wearing out the flesh of our body in the pursuit of pleasure; we
are under like obligation to treat the soul with care, to take fore-
thought for the quickness of the mind, to be sure that our speech is
not callous, but helpful, and never trifling. Whenever we fail to meet
our obligations, even those owed by ourselves to ourselves, the heav-
ier does our debt become.

3   Beyond all these debts, since we are, above all else, a creation
and formation of God, we are obliged to preserve a particular

disposition toward him, namely love "with all our heart, and with all our strength and with all our mind" (Mk 12.30). Should we not succeed in this we remain debtors of God, sinning against the Lord. And who shall pray for us in this case? For "should a person sin against another person when sinning, then they shall pray for him. But should he sin against the Lord, who will pray for him?" as Eli says in the first book of Kingdoms (1 Kg 2.25). We are, moreover, indebted to Christ who has purchased us with his own blood, just as a domestic slave is indebted to his purchaser for the sum that has been given for him. We are also indebted to the Holy Spirit, by whom we are marked for a day of redemption (cf. Eph 4.30), a debt we pay when we do not cause him grief. We cause him no grief when we bear the fruit required of us, as he is present with us and gives life to the soul. Even if we do not precisely know the identity of our individual angel, who looks upon the face of the Father in heaven (Mt 18.10), it is nonetheless clear to each of us, on examination, that we are likewise debtors to him in some respects. And insofar as the world is a theater of angels and humans, we should know that just as anyone in a theater is under obligation to say or to do certain things in sight of the spectators, and that he is punished as having affronted the whole theater should he fail to do them, so we too are under obligation to the whole world, to all the angels as to the human race, with regard to that which, should we be willing, we may learn from wisdom.

4   Apart from these more general debts, there is also that owed to a widow who is supported by the church,[70] and another to a deacon, and another to a presbyter, and the heaviest is that owed to a bishop,[71] for it is demanded by the Savior of the whole church, and recompense is due should he not repay it. As already noted, the apostle mentions the mutual debt of husband and wife when he says:

[70]The Christian community frequently gave widows economic support, as often they were left without economic support. They would support the church in turn through their prayer.

[71]A similar statement is made at *Homily on Jeremiah* 11.

"Let the husband pay his debt to his wife, and the wife likewise to the husband" (1 Cor 7.3), to which he adds, "Do not defraud one another" (1 Cor 7.5). But what need is there for me to speak of the extent of our debts, for which we shall be detained should we not repay, or set free should we repay them, when readers of this book may gather this for themselves from what has been said. Suffice it to say that it is impossible in this life to be free of debt at any hour of night or day.

5   When somebody is in debt, he either pays or withholds the obligation. And as it is possible to pay in a lifetime, it is possible also to withhold payment. There are some who owe nothing to anybody, some who owe a little, having repaid the greater part, and some who owe the greater part, having repaid a small amount. A person may conceivably owe everything, having repaid nothing. Somebody who has repaid everything in an attempt to be free of debt may achieve this in time, as he begs remission for his former debts,[72] and somebody who earnestly seeks to be regarded in this manner may achieve this in time, and so no debt will remain from his prior obligation. Lawless actions may leave their mark on the mind,[73] and become indictments against us on the basis of which we might be tried, which may be produced as evidence when we come to trial and are arraigned before the judgment seat of Christ as though they were confessions written by ourselves. So we shall each be rewarded in accordance with whatever we have done through the body, whether good or bad. It is of such debts that it is said in Proverbs: "If you have regard for yourself, do not give yourself as surety. For if he has not the ability to pay, they shall take away your bed from beneath you" (Prov 22.26–27).

6   But if we are indebted to so many, assuredly some are indebted to us. For some are indebted to us as human beings, others as fellow-citizens, others as to fathers, or as to sons and, beyond these, wives are indebted to husbands, and friends to friends. Therefore, when

---

[72]In other words, there is still guilt to be forgiven on the grounds of former debt.
[73]Cf. *On First Principles* 2.10.4.

any of those many who are indebted to us are remiss in making repayment of what is due to us, we should act the more kindly and bear no grudge toward them, remembering our own indebtedness, and how frequently we have defaulted, not only toward other people but also to God himself. Should we remember how we have been debtors, and have not repaid but have withheld, as the time in which we should have done something or other for our neighbor has elapsed, we shall be the more easy-going toward those who are indebted to us and have not repaid the debt. This will be the case especially if we are not forgetful of our transgressions against the divine, and the unrighteousness against the Most High that we may have spoken, whether out of ignorance of the truth or out of displeasure at the circumstances that have befallen us.

7   Now if we refuse to become more easy-going toward those who are indebted to us, we shall suffer that undergone by the person who did not remit the hundred denarii to his fellow-slave. Although, according to the parable as it is stated in the Gospel, he had previously been pardoned, the master deals severely with him, and exacts what had previously been remitted, and says: "Wicked and idle servant! Should you not have pitied your fellow slave just as I pitied you? Throw him in prison until he pays everything that he owes." The Lord adds to this: "So will the heavenly Father deal with you unless you each forgive your brother from your heart" (cf. Mt 18.30–35). When they say that they repent we should forgive those who have sinned against us, however often our debtor does this. For he says: "If your brother sin against you seven times a day, and seven times turns round and says: 'I repent,' you shall forgive him" (Lk 17.4). It is not for us to be harsh to those who are unrepentant, but rather these people are wicked to themselves, for "whoever refuses instruction hates himself" (Prov 15.32). Rather we should make every effort to bring healing to such people, who are so utterly perverted that they are incapable of perceiving their own downfall but are drunk with a drunkenness more fatal than wine, brought about through the darkening of evil.

8   Luke, when he says "Forgive us our sins," means the same as Matthew, for sins are brought about when we have debts and do not pay them. And he does not seem to yield a place to anyone who wishes to forgive only those debtors who are penitent, for he says that the Savior legislates that we should add to our prayer: "as we ourselves pardon everyone indebted to us." That we all have the authority to forgive sins against ourselves is clear from the words "as we also have forgiven our debtors" and "as we ourselves pardon everyone indebted to us." Yet whoever has been breathed upon by Jesus, like the apostles, and when, by his fruits, it can be known that he has received the Holy Spirit and is become spiritual through being led by the Spirit in the manner of a son of God in the performance of every duty which the word dictates, he forgives whatever God forgives, and retains whatever sins cannot be cured; and so, just as the prophets served God in speaking not their own words but those of the divine will, he likewise serves the God who alone has authority to forgive.

9   The language in the Gospel according to John, which concerns the forgiveness exercised by the apostles, is as follows: "Receive the Holy Spirit. Whoever's sins you forgive are forgiven them; whoever's sins you retain are retained" (Jn 20.22–23). Anyone who took this without examination might hold it against the apostles that they did not forgive all, so that all might be forgiven, but that they retained the sins of some, and that on their account they were likewise retained by God. In order to understand forgiveness of human sins by God through people it is helpful to take an example from the law. The priests, according to the law, were forbidden to offer sacrifice on account of certain sins, so that the person for whom the sacrifices were made might have those misdeeds forgiven. And whereas the priest has a certain authority to offer sacrifices for involuntary misdeeds,[74] he would never presume to offer a burnt offering and a sin

---

[74]This is the reading of the manuscript. Koetschau indicates in a footnote that he would prefer: "for involuntary or voluntary misdeeds."

offering in cases of adultery, or willful murder, or some other serious offense. In the same way the apostles, and those who may be compared to the apostles, those who are priests in the order of the great high-priesthood in that they have gained knowledge of God's healing process, come to know, as they are taught by the Spirit, the sins for which they ought to offer sacrifice, and when to do so, and in what manner, and recognize the sins for which they should not so do. And so Eli the priest, knowing that his sons Hophni and Phineas were sinners and sensing his inability to work with them toward the remission of their sins, confesses his despair of such an outcome as he says: "Should a person sin against another person when sinning, then they shall pray for him. But should he sin against the Lord, who will pray for him?" (1 Kg 2.25).

10 How I do not know, but there are those who have taken to themselves authority beyond the priestly dignity, perhaps because they have no accurate knowledge of the priesthood, and boast of their ability to pardon idolatry and to remit adultery and fornication, as though sin which leads to death might be absolved through their prayer on behalf of those who have dared commit these acts.[75] For they do not read the text: "There is sin which leads to death; I do not say that anyone should ask about it" (1 Jn 5.16). Nor should we be silent concerning the most valiant Job, who offers sacrifice on behalf of his sons saying: "Perhaps my sons have had evil thoughts toward God in their hearts" (Job 1.5). He offers sacrifice even though there is some doubt whether sin has been committed, and although nothing has reached as far as the lips.

---

[75]Certain sins, notably idolatry, adultery, and murder, were widely held as excluding a person from the church for their lifetimes, but in the third century, as we may observe in the controversies which met Cyprian, there was some development in the penitential system. It is possible that Origen is alluding to a similar practice to that known in Africa, by which potential martyrs claim, by their prayers, to be able to reinstate one who has lapsed into idolatry under persecution. For a more general discussion of this passage, together with a treatment of the rite of penance as described in Origen's works, see Joseph A. Favazza, *The Order of Penitents* (Collegeville MN: Liturgical Press, 1988), 147–163.

29

1   "And do not bring us into testing, but rescue us from evil." The phrase "but rescue us from evil" is omitted in Luke. Assuming that the Savior is not charging us to pray for the impossible, it seems to me to be worthwhile to explore how it is that we are ordered to request that we enter not into testing when the whole of human life is a time of testing. For while we are on earth we are in testing as we are surrounded with the flesh, which is at war against the spirit, whose mind is hostile to God since it is in no way able to be subject to the law of God.

2   We learn from Job that the whole of human life on earth is a time of testing, in these words: "For is not human life on earth a time of testing" (Job 7.1). The same is made plain by the seventeenth Psalm, in the words: "I shall be delivered from a time of testing in you" (Ps 17.30). Paul likewise, writing to the Corinthians, says that God does not grant that we escape testing, but that we should not be tested beyond our limits. He says: "No more than human testing has possessed you; God is faithful, and will not allow you to be tested beyond your limits. Rather, he provides a means of escape together with the testing, so that you will be able to bear it" (1 Cor 10.13). So whether we wrestle with the flesh, whose desires are at war with the spirit, or with the "soul of all flesh" (Lev 17.11), which is synonymous with the governing faculty, otherwise called the heart, which inhabits the body, for such is the wrestling undergone by those who are tested with human testing, or whether, as more advanced and more mature athletes who no longer wrestle against flesh and blood and who are bothered no more by human testing, as they have trodden them underfoot, we compete against "principalities and powers and the rulers of this world of darkness and the spiritual forces of wickedness" (Eph 6.12), we have no release from testing.

3   How then does the Savior command us to pray that we might not enter into testing when God tests everyone in some way? "For,"

says Judith,[76] not only to the elders of that time but to all who happen to read her book, "remember what he did to Abraham, and how he tested Isaac, and what happened to Jacob in Mesopotamia in Syria, while he was shepherd to the flocks of Laban, his mother's brother. Just as he tried them with fire in order to examine their hearts, so the Lord, who scourges those who approach him so that they may be admonished, is now not taking vengeance on us" (Jdt 8.26–27). And David shows that this is universally true for all the righteous when he says: "The afflictions of the righteous are many" (Ps 33.20), as does the apostle in Acts: "To enter the Kingdom of God we must pass through many afflictions" (Acts 14.22).

4   And unless we understand what many do not notice with regard to the request that we enter not into testing, we would have to say that the apostles were not heard when they prayed. For they suffered so much throughout their lives; "abounding in toil, abounding in blows, countlessly imprisoned, frequently in danger of death" (2 Cor 11.23). Paul alone received "forty strokes less one" five times at the hands of the Jews, was three times beaten with rods, was stoned once, was shipwrecked three times, passing "a day and a night in the deep" (2 Cor 11.23–25). He was a man set about by troubles "on every side," was impoverished and persecuted and cast down (2 Cor 4.8–9), as he confessed: "Even up to this present time we are hungry and thirsty and naked and beaten and homeless as we labor and work with our own hands. As we are reviled, we bless. As we are persecuted we accept it. As we are insulted we exhort" (1 Cor 4.11–13). If the apostles did not obtain what they sought when they prayed, what hope is there for their inferiors to be heard by God when they pray?

5   The statement in the twenty-fifth Psalm, "examine me, Lord, and test me, purify my kidneys and my heart with fire" (Ps 25.2), might easily be taken, by those who do not carefully examine the intention of the Savior's command, as being diametrically opposed to what our Lord taught concerning prayer. Who might ever think

[76]A suggestion of Anglus. The manuscript reads "The Jewish woman, if . . ."

that people were outside the scope of testing, when he has experience of them and has attained reason? And on what occasion might anyone be confident of having no need to struggle against the commission of sin? Should anyone be poor? He should take good care not to steal and to swear by the name of God (Prov 30.9b). Or rich? He has no grounds of confidence, for he can become utterly false and say in his exaltation: "Who sees me?" (Prov 30.9a) Not even Paul, who was rich "in all speech and in all knowledge" (1 Cor 1.5) was relieved of the possibility that he might sin through exalting himself because of these, but was in need of Satan's goad to beat him, so that he would not become overly exalted (2 Cor 12.7). And even should a person be of good conscience in himself, and fly away from evil, he should read what is said in the second book of Chronicles concerning Hezekiah, who is said to have fallen "through the haughtiness in his heart" (2 Chr 32.25–26).

6   And if anyone were confident of avoiding testing on the grounds of poverty, because I have not said much concerning poor people, he should know that the plotter is plotting to "overthrow the beggar and the poor" (Ps 36.14), especially since, according to Solomon, "the beggar tolerates no threat" (Prov 13.8). Yet what need is there to relate how many have found a place of punishment alongside the rich man in the Gospel on the grounds of their failure properly to administer their material wealth? And how many have fallen away from their hope of heaven through bearing ignobly their poverty, behaving in a manner more servile and dishonorable than is fitting for the saints. Not even those who are between these extremes of wealth and poverty escape from sin on the grounds of their moderate possessions.

7   But somebody who is healthy in body and strong might assume that he is immune from any testing on the grounds of his health and strength alone. Yet who would dare say, since the meaning of the passage is so obvious to all, that anyone apart from the healthy and strong is prone to the sin of defiling the temple of God (1 Cor 3.17). And who, lying sick, has escaped the incitements to defile the temple

of God, since at such a time he is idle, and highly receptive to thoughts of impurity. And what need is there to speak of what might trouble him apart from these, unless he guard his heart with all vigilance (Prov 4.23). For many who are overcome by troubles, and who know not how to bear illness bravely, are shown to be sick in soul, rather than in body. And many have fallen into eternal shame since they have fled dishonor, and have been ashamed nobly to bear the name of Christ.

8   Someone might think that, when he receives human approval, he has a respite from testing. And yet is it not a hard saying which is proclaimed to those who are haughty on account of the approval which is theirs from the many: "Their reward they have received from people" (Mt 6.2). And is not the saying: "How can you believe when you receive honor from each other, and do not seek honor from God alone?" (Jn 5.44). And why should I make a list of the crimes done in pride by the nobility, and the fawning submission of the so-called low-born toward those who, in their ignorance, they consider their betters, which distances from God those without true friendship, who dissemble love, which is the finest of human attributes.[77]

9   As has already been said, "the whole of human life on earth is testing" (Job 7.1). Let us pray, therefore, that we be delivered from testing, not so that we should not be tested (for this is impossible, in particular for those who are on earth), but so that we should not be overcome when we are tested. I understand somebody who is overcome when tested as entering "into" testing, becoming entangled in its nets. Into these nets the Savior entered on account of those who were previously caught within them, and "peering out through the nets," as it is said in the Song of Songs, answers those who previously were caught within them and have entered into testing, and speaks to those who are become his bride: "Arise, come, my dear one, my fair one, my dove" (Song 2.9–10). For further demonstration that no

---

[77]"Friendship," in the ancient world, would often refer to the duties of patronage, which would include flattery and false praise offered in order to gain some benefit.

occasion is free of testing for humanity, I will add that even someone who meditates on the law of God "day and night" (Ps 1.2) and
seeks conformity to the saying "the mouth of the just shall meditate
wisdom" (Prov 10.31), is not immune from testing.

10   I need not say how many, in devoting themselves to the study of
the divine Scriptures, have misinterpreted what is said in the law and
prophets and so devoted themselves to godless and impious doctrines which are foolish and ridiculous, since so many fail in this way,
even though they do not seem to be open to the charge of careless
reading. The same has been experienced by many readers of the
apostolic writings and of the Gospels, for in their lack of discernment they have fashioned another son, or a father, apart from those
described divinely and known to the saints in accordance with the
truth. For whoever does not understand the truth concerning God
or his Christ has fallen away from the true God and his only begotten. The being constructed out of foolishness, thought to be father
or son, he does not truly worship, and this has occurred through failure to recognize the testing which lurks in the reading of holy Scripture, and so does not stand armed for the struggle in which he has
enlisted.

11   Therefore we should pray not that we should not be tested, for
this is impossible, but that we should not be engulfed by testing, for
those who are in its midst are so overcome. Since it is written, apart
from the Prayer, ". . . that you do not enter into testing" (Lk 22.40),
the meaning of which is surely clear from what has already been said,
whereas in the Prayer we should say to God our Father, "Do not
bring us into testing," it is worthwhile seeing how we should think
of God as leading someone who has not prayed, or one whose prayer
has not been heard, into testing. For it is incongruous to think, when
somebody enters into testing and is overcome, that God himself
leads anyone into testing, as though handing him over for conquest.
And the same incongruity awaits anyone who attempts to interpret
the words: "Pray that you do not enter into testing." For since falling
into testing is an evil thing, on account of which we pray that we

should not undergo it, is it not unreasonable to suppose that the good God, who is incapable of bringing forth bad fruit, might engulf anyone in evils?

12   It would be useful in this regard to compare with these passages what is said to the Romans by Paul: "Professing themselves wise they turned to foolishness, and exchanged the glory of the incorruptible God for the likeness of an image of a corruptible mortal, and of birds and of quadrupeds and of creeping things. Therefore God handed them over to impurity in the desires of their hearts, so that they might dishonor their bodies among themselves" (Rom 1.22–24). And a little later: "Therefore God handed them over to the passions of dishonor. The women then exchanged their natural functions for those contrary to nature, and the men likewise set aside the natural relationship with women and were consumed . . ." and the rest (Rom 1.26–27). And again, a little further on: "Just as they proved to have no cognizance of God, so God handed them over to having a corrupt mind, so that they would act improperly" (Rom 1.28). With all these passages we should confront those who divide the divinity, who consider the good Father of our Lord to be distinct from the God of the law.[78] Does not the good God lead anyone who fails in prayer into testing? Does not the Father of the Lord hand those who have sinned in any way over to impurity in the desires of their hearts, so that they might dishonor their bodies among themselves? And since, as they say, he is relieved of judging and punishing, does he hand them over to passions of dishonor, and to a corrupt mind, so that they would act improperly, even though they would not be in the desires of their hearts, unless they were handed over to them by

---

[78]Here Origen makes explicit reference to the Marcionites. Marcionites held that the God of the Old Testament, who had given the law with its consequent condemnation for those who do not keep it, was a different God from the God of the New Testament who was the father of Jesus. The point of the following series of rhetorical questions (which, in Greek, is one long rhetorical question) is to point out that the Lord taught that we should pray to his Father not to be delivered into testing. The stress on the goodness of God in the next section is likewise an allusion to the Marcionites, who distinguished the just God of the Old Testament from the good God of the New.

God? And would not be mired in passions of dishonor had God not handed them over? And would not have lapsed into a corrupt mind had God not handed over those who were so condemned?

13   I am well aware that these passages trouble them greatly, and that on this account they have fashioned another God apart from the one who made the heaven and the earth, since they found many such passages in the law and the prophets and have determined that anyone who utters such words cannot be good. Having already faced difficulties deriving from the phrase: "Do not bring us into testing," and on this account having cited the apostolic pronouncements, we must now consider whether worthwhile solutions to the incongruities are to be found. I do think that God deals with each rational soul in such a way as to lead it to eternal life, though it always possesses free will and on its own account may ascend to the summit of goodness through the better things, or may otherwise descend to a certain degree on account of heedlessness to the extent of wickedness. Accordingly, since a speedy and rapid cure may bring about contempt in some people for the disease into which they have fallen, so that they contract it a second time after regaining their health, so he may, in such cases, reasonably allow the evil to increase, allowing it so to augment within them as to be incurable, so that wallowing in the evil for a long time and being surfeited with the sin after which they longed, they may be sated and be made aware of the harm they have done to themselves, and so learn to hate what formerly they had welcomed, so that when they are healed they may enjoy more steadfastly the health which has come to their souls through their healing.

So it was for the mixed throng among the children of Israel. Their desire was great, and they and the children of Israel sat and wept, saying: "Who will give us meat to eat? We remember the fish that we ate freely in Egypt, and the cucumbers and the melons and the leeks and the onions and the garlic. But now our soul is parched, for our eyes look on nothing but this manna" (Num 11.4–6). Then shortly afterward it is said: "And Moses heard them crying in their families; each was at his door" (Num 11.10). And again, a little later, the Lord says to Moses: "Say this to the people: 'Sanctify yourselves for tomorrow, and you shall eat meat, because you have cried out before the Lord saying: "Who will give us meat to eat? For it went well for us in Egypt." And the Lord will give you meat to eat, and you will eat meat. Not for one day only will you eat it, nor for two, nor for five, nor for ten days, nor for twenty days. For a month you will eat it, until it is coming out of your nostrils. It will become loathsome to you, because you have disobeyed the Lord who is among you, and have cried out before him and said: "Why did we come out of Egypt?"'"

14   Let us see, therefore, whether the narrative which I have laid out may usefully be applied to a solution of the difficulty in the clause "Do not bring us into testing," and in the statements of the apostolic writings.

Having desires and longing, the mixed throng among the children of Israel, and the children of Israel with them, wept. It is clear that as long as they did not possess what they desired they would have no satisfaction, and their passions would not cease. But the merciful and good God, in granting their desire, did not wish to grant it in such a way that their desire might continue in them. Therefore he says that they should eat meat not for one day only, for should they have partaken of the meat for a short while their passion would remain and the soul be kindled and inflamed by it. Nor does he grant them what they desired for two days. Since he willed that they should be surfeited with it, he utters what, to anyone who understands, is actually a threat, though it seemed gratifying to them: "You shall not spend five days only eating meat, nor twice that, nor even twice that, but you shall spend a whole month eating meat, until that which you thought so good is coming out of your nostrils, together with your loathsome passion, and your culpable and base desire. In this way will I release you from desires in your lives, so that when you emerge you may be pure from all desires, and remember the suffering that you underwent in order to be released from it. So you will be unable ever to fall into it again or, should this happen due to forgetfulness after long intervals of time of the sufferings you underwent on account of your desire, should you fail to assimilate to yourselves the word which perfectly releases you from every passion, should you subsequently fall into evil and desire earthly things again and beg a second time to obtain those things which you presently desire, you will come to hate what you desire, and so hurry back to good things, and to the heavenly nourishment so despised by those who long for wickedness."

15   It will go similarly for those who exchange "the glory of the incorruptible God for the likeness of an image of a corruptible mortal, and of birds and of quadrupeds and of creeping things," who on this account have been abandoned and handed over "to impurity in the desires of their hearts, so that they might dishonor their bodies," who have ascribed to a body without intelligence or feeling the name of the one who has bestowed on all sentient and rational creatures not sense alone but rational sense, and to some the grace of a completely admirable ability to sense and to reason. It is reasonable that such people should be handed over by God to the passions of dishonor, that they should be forsaken of him whom they had abandoned, and that they should receive the reward of their error, by which they came to love the itch for pleasure. It is a better reward for their error to be handed over to the passions of dishonor than that they should be purified by the fire of wisdom, than that they be imprisoned and their debts exacted from them to the very last cent (Mt 18.34). For when they are given up to the passions of dishonor, not only to those which are natural but also to many which are unnatural, they are debased and coarsened by the flesh as though they were no longer in possession of soul or mind but become entirely flesh, whereas they do not receive the reward of their error in the fire and in the prison, but a beneficial purification of the evils which in their error they had contracted alongside the love of pleasure, together with salutary suffering, and are so set free from the filth and the blood in which they were mired and defiled, so that, being so close to destruction, they could not even consider salvation.

So shall God wash away the filth from the sons and daughters of Zion, and shall purify them from the blood in their midst with the spirit of judgment and the spirit of burning (Is 4.4). For he comes like a refining fire and like cleansing soap (Mal 3.2), cleansing and purifying those who are in need of such remedies because, when they were tried, they preferred not to retain a knowledge of God. When they have been treated by such remedies they will come to despise the corrupt mind, for God desires that people should attain the good not under compulsion but willingly. It is possible that, through long exposure to evil, some will have difficulty perceiving its baseness, yet will turn away from it, since they falsely perceive that it is precious.

16   Give some thought, moreover, to whether this is the reason why God hardened the heart of Pharaoh, namely so that he would not be able to say, because he was hardened, what he did indeed say: "The Lord is just, but I and my people are irreligious" (Ex 9.27). But he was in need of greater hardening, and of further suffering, so that he would not simply regard the hardening as an evil and so be deserving of a hardening many times worse, as the result ceasing to be hardened too speedily. If, as Proverbs says, "It is not unjust that nets be spread for birds" (Prov 1.17), then God quite rightly leads us "into the snare" (as in the statement, "You led us into the snare" [Ps 65.11]). Not even the cheapest of birds, a sparrow, falls into a snare without the Father willing it, for its falling into the snare comes about on account of its failure to make proper use of the power of its wings, which were given so that it might soar upward;[79] and so let us pray that we should do nothing that would make us worthy of being led into testing through God's just judgment. For everyone who is handed over to impurity by God in the desires of his own heart is so led, as is everyone who is handed over to the passions of dishonor, and everyone who does not prove to have God in himself is handed over to a corrupt mind, to do whatever is improper.

[79]Apart from the obvious reference to Lk 12.6, there is a reference to Plato's myth of the winged soul in *Phaedrus* here.

17   The utility of testing is thus something like this: through testing the things which our souls have admitted, unknown to anyone except God, unknown even to ourselves, are made manifest, so that we should no longer be unaware of what kind of people we are, but may recognize this and, should we so wish, perceive our own evil and give thanks for the good things which have been made manifest to us through the testing. It is set forth by the Lord in Job, and is written in Deuteronomy, that testing comes upon us so that our true nature may be revealed to ourselves, and so that we may discern what is hidden in our hearts. The passages are as follow: "Do you think that I should have answered you except to reveal you as righteous" (Job 40.3) and, in Deuteronomy: "He afflicted you and starved you and fed you with manna, and he led you astray in the desert, where there were biting snakes and scorpions and drought, so that what was in your heart might be made known" (Deut 8.3, 15, 2).

18   If only we would recall the story, we would know that Eve's readiness to be deceived and the corruption of her reasoning did not come about when she disobeyed God and listened to the serpent but already existed and then came to the fore, which is the reason why the serpent approached her, since it had perceived her weakness through its own cunning (Gen 3.1ff). Nor did evil originate in Cain when he killed his brother, for God, who knows our hearts, had no regard for Cain or for his offerings (Gen 4.5), but his wickedness became obvious when he murdered Abel. If Noah had not drunk the wine that he had cultivated, and become intoxicated and exposed himself, neither the rashness and disrespect of Ham toward his father nor the respect and modesty of his brothers toward their parent would have been revealed (Gen 9.20–24). And Esau's plot against Jacob might seem to have provided sufficient pretext for the removal of his blessing, yet already his soul had the roots of fornication and profanity (Heb 12.16). And we should not have known the shining example of Joseph's continence, fortified as he was against the onslaught of any urging, had not the wife of his master fallen in love with him (Gen 39.7ff).

19   Therefore, in the intervals between successive tests, let us stand
fast against those that are to come, and be prepared for all possible
future outcomes, so that we shall not stand convicted of unreadiness
but be known to be carefully forearmed. For when we have done all
that is in our power, God will make up whatever is lacking through
our human weakness as he works together with those who love him
for good in all things (Rom 8.28), since in accordance with his
inerrant foreknowledge he has foreseen what they shall come to be.

30

1   It seems to me that Luke, in his "Do not bring us into testing"
has also taught us the meaning of "rescue us from evil." It is indeed
natural that the Lord should have spoken the summary form to the
disciple, as he had already[80] received assistance, whereas the more
explicit is addressed to the majority, who were in need of clearer
instruction. God does not rescue us from evil when we are not under
attack from the enemy opposing us by whatever means are at his disposal, or by whichever ministers of his will, but when we make a
brave stand against these contingencies, and are victorious. I have
expounded the words "The afflictions of the righteous are many, and
he rescues them from them all" (Ps 33.20) in this way, for God rescues from afflictions not by preventing such affliction, for when Paul
says "afflicted on every side" (2 Cor 4.8) he means that he is still
afflicted, but when, through the help of God, we are afflicted but not
distressed. Affliction, according to the tradition of the Hebrews,
denotes misfortune which occurs against one's will, whereas distress
is a matter of disposition whilst under affliction, being overcome by
it, and giving in. And so Paul quite rightly says: "We are afflicted on
every side but not distressed." I reckon that this verse in the Psalms
is of like meaning: "You enlarged me in affliction" (Ps 4.2). For
our cheerfulness and contentment through the cooperation and

---

[80]Reading here *hēdē*, instead of the *dē* of the manuscript.

presence of the encouraging and saving word of God in the time of misfortune is termed "enlargement."

2   It is in a similar manner that we are to think of rescue from evil. God rescued Job not because the devil had not received the power to set him about with various tests, for he received it, but because he did not sin before the Lord in all that happened to him, but exhibited his righteousness. So he was put to shame for uttering falsehood against Job when he said: "Does Job fear the Lord for nothing? Have you not encircled him, and whatever is in his house, and whatever he has which is outside his house, and blessed his deeds and made his herds abound upon the earth? Yet stretch forth your hand and touch whatever he has, and will he not curse you to your face?" (Job 1.9–11). For after so much suffering he did not, as the adversary said, curse God to his face, but continued to bless the Lord even after he was handed over to the tester, and reproached his wife when she said: "Speak against the Lord and die." He rebuked her and said: "You are talking like one of the senseless women. If we have received good things from the Lord's hand, should we not bear the evil" (Job 2.9–10).

And the devil spoke to the Lord concerning Job a second time. "Skin for skin. All that a person possesses will he pay for his life. But stretch forth your hand and touch his bones and his flesh, and will he not curse you to your face?" (Job 2.4–5). But he is conquered by the champion of virtue and proved a liar. For he remained faithful and committed no sin with his lips before the Lord, even though he suffered the severest difficulties. Job wrestled two bouts, and won, but did not have to contest such a struggle three times, for it was reserved for the Savior to wrestle three times, as is recorded in the three Gospels, when our Savior, known in his humanity, three times triumphed over the enemy (Mt 4.1–11 & par.).

3   Therefore, in order to ask God with understanding not to enter not into testing and that we be rescued from evil, we might examine these things and investigate them carefully among ourselves, and so be worthy of a hearing through listening to God. And let us implore

him when we are tested that we be not brought to death, and that when we are assaulted by the fiery darts of the evil one (Eph 6.16) we be not set on fire by them. Now those who are set on fire by them are all those whose hearts, according to one of the twelve (prophets), are like a baking pot (Hos 7.6). Those who douse with the shield of faith all the fiery darts that are launched at them by the evil one are not set on fire. Within themselves they have rivers of water springing up for everlasting life (Jn 4.14) which do not allow the fire of the evil one to spread,[81] but readily bring it to nothing through the flood of the inspired and saving thoughts which are impressed on the soul of the one who aspires to be spiritual from the contemplation of the truth.

31

After this, it seems to me that this is not the wrong place to add some rather elementary comments concerning the disposition and posture that we should have in praying, concerning the place where we should pray, and the direction in which we should look, apart from in exceptional circumstances, and the time which is suitable and marked out for prayer, and any similar point, so to complete the discussion of the issue of prayer.

1   Disposition is a matter of the soul, and posture of the body. Now Paul, as we said above,[82] was describing disposition when he says that we should pray without anger and without dissent, but posture in "Lifting up holy hands" (1 Tim 2.8). This seems to me to have been taken from the Psalms, where it says: "The lifting up of my hands as an evening sacrifice" (Ps 140.2). Concerning place, "I desire that men pray in every place" (1 Tim 2.8). And concerning direction, in the Wisdom of Solomon: "Thus is it known that we should precede the sun to give thanks to you, and to plead with you before the dawning of the light" (Wis 16.28).

[81]The word "fire" does not appear in the manuscript and is added following Anglus.
[82]At 9.1.

2   Accordingly it seems to me that anyone who intends to embark on prayer should lay a foundation for himself by preparing himself a while so that he will be the more attentive and alert throughout his prayer. He will have put aside every testing and troubling thought and will recall, as far as possible, the greatness of the one whom he is approaching, and the disrespect which lies in approaching him yawning and inattentively and, as it were, contemptuously. He will put aside all alien thoughts, so coming to prayer, extending his soul, as it were, before extending his hands, his mind intent on God before his eyes and, before standing, raising his intellect from the earth and setting it before the Lord of all. All remembrance of wrongs against anyone who is supposed to have done him injustice should be put away, as much as he would that God have no remembrance against himself should he have done injustice, or sinned against any of his neighbors, or be conscious of having acted contrary to right reason.

Nor can there be any doubt that, of the numerous dispositions of the body, standing with hands extended and eyes upraised is much to be preferred, in that one thereby wears on the body the image of the characteristics which are becoming to the soul in prayer. I say that all of this should be observed by preference, apart from any exceptional circumstance. For under certain circumstances we may quite properly pray sitting down, because of an unbearable disorder of the foot, or even lying down, because of a fever or some such ailment, and on occasion, let us say we are on a voyage, or our business does not permit us to retire to pay our debt of prayer, we may pray without any outward indication that we are so doing.

3   Yet we should know that kneeling, because it is a symbol of humility and submission, is essential when one intends to confess ones own sins against God and to beseech healing for them, and remission. As Paul says: "For this reason I bow my knees to the Father, after whom the whole family of heaven and earth is named" (Eph 3.14–15). It appears to me that in the phrase: ". . . in the name of Jesus every knee should bow, in heaven and on earth and under the

earth" (Phil 2.10), the apostle indicates rational kneeling, which means that each being has humbled itself, falling before God "in the name of Jesus." For we should not suppose that heavenly beings have bodies so fashioned that they have corporeal knees, for their bodies have been shown to be spherical by those who have made accurate examination of these matters.[83] If anyone refuses to admit this, unless he shamelessly refuses to see reason, he will have to admit that each member has its use, and that nothing will have been pointlessly formed in them by God. In either event he falls into error, whether in asserting that bodily members have been made by God pointlessly, and not with their own proper function, or in stating that there are internal organs, even the rectum, which perform their particular function in the heavenly places! To reason that, as with statues, there is only the surface appearance of a human, and nothing inside, would be extremely foolish.

This occurs to me in examining the question of kneeling, and seeing that "In the name of Jesus every knee shall bow, in heaven and on earth and under the earth." But what is written in the prophet, "Every knee shall bow to me" (Is 45.23), is the same.

4   With regard to place, we should know that every place is rendered fit for prayer by one who prays aright, for " 'Offer sacrifice to me in every place' says the Lord" (Mal 1.11), and "I desire that men pray in every place" (1 Tim 2.8). But to arrange the performance of prayer in quiet, and without distraction, each person should select, if possible, what one might term the most appropriate place in his house, and so to pray. Beyond the general examination of the place, he should consider whether any law has been broken, or anything contrary to right reason has been done in the place in which he is praying. Otherwise he might make not only himself but also the place of his prayer such that the regard of God might shun it.

As I give further consideration to this matter of place, I am led to express an opinion which, though it may be harsh, nonetheless

---

[83]Plato *Timaeus* 33B; Aristotle *On the Soul* 1.2.

should not be disregarded by anyone who studies it carefully; namely whether it is holy and pure to entreat God in the place of intercourse, which is not unlawful but, in accordance with the apostle's saying, is "by indulgence, and not injunction" (1 Cor 7.6). For if it is not possible to allow time for prayer in the manner in which one should pray, except by devoting oneself to it "by consent, for a period" (1 Cor 7.5) perhaps we should give due reflection to whether the place is fitting.

5   A place of prayer that has a particular blessing and benefit is the place where believers gather. It seems probable that angelic powers are in attendance at the assemblies of the faithful, as well as the power of the Lord and Savior himself, and indeed holy spirits—I think of those who have gone to their rest before us. It is clear that they are around us who continue in life, even if it is difficult to say precisely how. With regard to angels we should reckon as follows: if "the angel of the Lord will encamp around those who fear him, and rescue them" (Ps 33.8), and Jacob, when he says "the angel rescues me from all evils" (Gen 48.16), speaks the truth not for himself alone but for all who devote themselves to God, who was with him,[84] it is reasonable to suppose, when several are gathered together in sincerity for the glory of Christ, that the angel, who is around any of those that fear, is around each of those who are with the man to whom he has been committed as guardian and guide. Thus when there is an assembly of those who are holy there is a twofold church, human and angelic. And if Raphael says that it is the prayer of Tobit alone that he has borne up as a remembrance (Tobit 12.13), and subsequently that of Sarah, who later became his daughter-in-law as a result of her marriage to Tobias, what are we to say when several who are of the same mind and share the same conviction come together and are made one body in Christ? And Paul speaks of the presence of the power of the Lord with the church: "When you are gathered with my spirit together with the power of the Lord Jesus" (1 Cor 5.4).

[84]Reading *sunonti* rather than the *sunienti* of the manuscript.

Not with the Ephesians alone is the power of the Lord Jesus united,[85] but with the Corinthians, and if Paul, while still clothed in the body, considers that his spirit is united with those at Corinth, we should not abandon the belief that in the same way those blessed ones who have departed are prominent at the church in spirit, perhaps more than anyone who is in the body. For which reason we should not think lightly of praying in them, for such prayers bestow a singular grace on any who joins in them with sincerity.

6   Just as the power of Jesus and the spirit of Paul and of those like him, and the angels of the Lord who encamp around each of the saints, combine and come together with those who assemble together in sincerity, so we may conjecture that should anyone be unworthy of a holy angel through sin and transgression in contempt of God, giving himself up to a devil's angel, as long as those like him be few, it shall not be long before such a person fails to escape the providence of the angels which watch over the church in the service of the divine will, which providence will make general knowledge of the misdeeds of such a person. Should such persons become numerous, and gather in the manner of human societies to conduct business of a material nature, they will not be watched over. This is made clear in Isaiah, as the Lord says: "Not even if you come to appear before me" (Is 1.12), for, he says, "I will turn my eyes away from you; even if you multiply your supplication I will not listen to you" (Is 1.15). For instead of the twofold company of holy people and blessed angels that was mentioned above, there may perhaps be a twofold combination of impious people and wicked angels. With regard to such a gathering, both holy angels and devout persons might say: "I have not sat down with the council of vanity, and I have not gone in with transgressors. I have hated the congregation of evildoers, and I will not sit with the impious" (Ps 25.4–5).

7   It was, I think, on this account that those in Jerusalem and the whole of Judaea have become subject to their enemies. For having

---

[85]The first letter to the Corinthians was written at Ephesus.

sinned extensively, and having become peoples that had abandoned the law, they were abandoned by God, and by defending angels, and by saintly men with their saving works. Thus whole assemblies are abandoned sometimes to fall into testing, and even what they seem to have is taken from them (Lk 8.18). Like the fig tree that gave no fruit to Jesus when he was hungry they are accursed and grubbed up by the roots (Mk 11.13ff), withering and losing whatever sustaining power they might once have had through faith. It seems to me that it was necessary to have said this in discussing the place of prayer, and in suggesting that it is preferable in that place where saintly persons meet, gathering reverently together as a congregation.

32

A few words may now be said on the direction that one should face whilst at prayer. Since there are four directions, toward the north and the south, and toward the rising of the sun and its setting, who would not immediately agree that the direction of sunrise obviously indicates that we should make our prayer facing in that direction, as having the symbolic implication that the soul is facing the rising of the true light? Should anyone desire to offer his petitions in the direction in which his house opens, whatever the direction in which the doorway faces, stating that the sight of heaven seems more inviting to him than a view of a wall,[86] and that the eastern side has no aperture, we should say that it is by artifice that peoples' buildings open up in one or another direction, whereas it is by nature that the direction of sunrise is to be favored above the remaining directions, and that the natural is to be upheld over the artificial. Indeed, if anyone desired to pray in open countryside, on this logic why should

[86]According to R Hiya b Abba (cited at Babylonian Talmud, *Berakoth* 34b), prayer should only be made in a room where there is a window. There may be a connection with the discussion here, as the practice of praying toward the east is in deliberate contradistinction to the Jewish practice of praying toward the Temple; notably Daniel's room (Dan 6.10) had a window that opened in that direction.

they pray toward the sunrise, rather than its setting? If it is reasonable there to favor the east, why should this not always be the case? And that is enough on that subject.[87]

33

1   I think that I should bring this treatise to its conclusion by treating the sections of prayer. It seems to me that four sections, which I have found distributed throughout the Scriptures, should be described, and that each prayer should be constructed in accordance with these sections. The divisions are as follow:

At the beginning of prayer, in a preface, glory should be ascribed to God according to one's ability, through Christ who is glorified with him, and in the Holy Spirit who is to be hymned with him.

After this we should each place thanksgiving, both general, enumerating all the benefits that are extended to so many, and for which thanks are given, and those particular blessings which each has personally received from God.

After thanksgiving, it seems to me that we should become a pungent accuser of our own sins before God, first so that we can ask healing, to be delivered from the disposition that instigates sin and second to gain forgiveness for past actions.

After confession, it seems to me that we should add in the fourth place petition for what is great and heavenly, for ourselves and for people in general, and also for our family and friends.

[87]Clement *Stromata* 7.7, is similarly peremptory on the necessity of praying toward the east, employing a similar logic. Cf., however, Origen *Homilies on Leviticus* 9.10, who with reference to Zech 6.12 and Mal 3.20, states that this is the direction from which salvation comes, as "east," in these texts, is an allegorical reference to Christ. Tertullian *Apology* 16.9–10 is another early witness to praying in an eastward direction. For discussion see F. Dölger, *Sol Salutis* (Münster: Aschendorff, 1920), 115–127, E. Peterson "Die geschichtliche Bedeutung der jüdischen Gebetsrichtung" in *Frühkirche, Judentum und Gnosis* (Rome: Herder, 1959), 1–14, and Willy Rordorf, "Les gestes accompagnant la prière d'après Tertullian *De oratione* 11–30, et Origène PERI EUCHÊS 31–32" in *Gestes et paroles dans les diverses familles liturgiques* (*Bibliotheca Ephemerides liturgicae* Subsidia 14; Rome: Centro liturgico Vincenziano, 1978), 191–203.

And every prayer should be brought to its conclusion with the glorification of God through Christ in the Holy Spirit.

2   As I have said, I have found these sections distributed throughout the scriptures. The ascription of glory in these words of the one hundred third psalm: "Lord, my God, how exceeding great you are. You have put on thanksgiving and majesty, being wrapped in light as with a garment, stretching out the heaven like a curtain, covering its upper story with waters, making clouds a chariot, walking on the wings of winds, making angels of its breath and ministers of flames of fire. He sets the earth on firm foundations, unfaltering for endless ages, with the deep as a covering garment, waters standing on the mountains. They shall flee at your rebuke, they shall shrink in fear from your thundering voice" (Ps 103.1–7). Indeed the greater part of this psalm consists of the glorification of the Father. Anyone may select for himself numerous passages and see how widely this section of glorification is distributed.

3   This may be cited as an example of thanksgiving. It is found in the second book of Kingdoms, and is uttered by David in astonishment at God's gift and giving thanks in these words, after the promises to David through Nathan: "Who am I, O Lord, my Lord, and what is my house, that you have loved me to such an extent? Indeed, I have shrunk very small in your sight, my Lord, yet you have spoken on behalf of your servant's house for a long time to come. This is the human law, O Lord, my Lord. And what should David go on to say to you? And now, Lord, you know your servant. You have done this on behalf of your servant, and in accordance with your heart you have done such great things, so that your servant should know that you should be magnified, O Lord my Lord" (2 Kg 7.18–22).

4   An example of confession is: "Rescue me from all my transgressions" (Ps 38.9). And elsewhere: "My wounds stink from corruption because of my folly. I am troubled and bowed down to the uttermost; all day I go around downcast" (Ps 37.6–7).

5   As a petition, note the twenty-seventh Psalm: "Do not lead me away with sinners, and do not wipe me out together with workers of wickedness" (Ps 27.3) and other similar passages.

6   It is right that we should begin with glorifying and leave off our prayer with glorifying, hymning and giving glory to the Father of all, through Jesus Christ in the Holy Spirit, to whom be glory for ever and ever.

34

Ambrosius and Tatiana, lovers of learning and sincerest kinfolk in devotion, I have struggled through my treatment of the question of prayer, of prayer in the Gospels and of the preface to that prayer in Matthew. I do not doubt that, if you stretch forth for that which is before, and forget whatever is behind, and in the meantime pray for me, I shall obtain from God the giver a more extensive and more divine capacity with which to discuss these matters again in a manner more noble, more exalted, and more lucid.

For the present, you will read this with indulgence.

We hope this book has been enjoyable and edifying for your spiritual journey toward our Lord and Savior Jesus Christ.

One hundred percent of the net proceeds of all SVS Press sales directly support the mission of St Vladimir's Orthodox Theological Seminary to train priests, lay leaders, and scholars to be active apologists of the Orthodox Christian Faith. However, the proceeds only partially cover the operational costs of St Vladimir's Seminary. To meet our annual budget, we rely on the generosity of donors who are passionate about providing theological education and spiritual formation to the next generation of ordained and lay servant leaders in the Orthodox Church.

 Donations are tax-deductible and can be made at www.svots.edu/donate. We greatly appreciate your generosity.

To engage more with St Vladimir's Orthodox Theological Seminary, please visit:

www.svots.edu
online.svots.edu
www.svspress.com
www.instituteofsacredarts.com

POPULAR PATRISTICS SERIES

ST VLADIMIR'S SEMINARY PRESS
1-800-204-2665 • www.svspress.com